THE INHERITED SILENCE

*HEALING EMOTIONAL WOUNDS AND
REDEFINING STRENGHT
(PART 1 OF THE UNHELD SERIES)*

GERALD E. O.

Table of Contents

WEEK 1: THE INHERITED SILENCE 10
WEEK 2: MASCULINITY 46
    Mindful Minute: 60
    DAY 11: The Performance of Power 63
    DAY 13: Defining Manhood for Yourself 73
    DAY 14: Coming Home to Yourself 79
WEEK 3: STRONG BUT NUMB 84
    DAY 15: Numb Isn't Neutral 84
    DAY 16: Where Does It Hurt? 89
    DAY 17: Feelings Aren't Facts — But They Matter 95
    DAY 18: You Can Be Both 100
    DAY 19: The Quiet Cost of Numbing 105
    DAY 20: Emotional Muscles 110
    DAY 21: The Truth Underneath 115
WEEK 4: THE PRESSURE OF PROVIDING 120
    Day 22: The Provider Script 120
    Day 25 – The Lie of Self-Sacrifice 135
    Day 29: The Things I Don't Say 156
    Day 31: The Unseen Grief 165
WEEK 6: GRIEF YOU NEVER CLAIMED 187
    Day 36: The Grief I Didn't Acknowledge 187
    Day 42: Honoring My Emotional Survival 218
WEEK 7: THE PROTECTOR REDEFINED 223
    Day 43: Redefining Strength 223
    Day 45: The Fear Beneath Protection 232
    Day 46: The Protector Within 236

Day 48: Safety over Secrecy 245
Day 50: Meet the Boy Again 255
Day 52: What Did He Need? 265
Day 57: More than Angry 287
Day 58: Expand the Vocabulary 292
Day 63: Words That Heal 315
Day 64: My Body Speaks 319
Day 65: Shoulders Down, Heart Open 323
Day 66: The Gut Feeling 327
Day 67: Breath as a Messenger 331
WEEK 11: I'M ALLOWED 349
Day 71: I'm Here 349
Day 75: Safe to Be Seen 366
WEEK 12: The Masculine Need for Affection 378
Day 78 – Starved for Softness 378
Day 81 – It's Not Always About Sex 391
Day 85: The Shame of Ambition 408
Day 88: The Fear of Outgrowing Others 423
Month 3 Reflection: Hidden Wins 437
WEEK 14: 442
How We've Been Taught to Abandon Ourselves 442
Day 92: When Pleasing Becomes Self-Erasure 442
Day 95: Seeking Validation Outside Myself 455
Day 98: Coming Home to Myself 467
Day 99: The Strength of Stillness 471

A Note to the Reader

This is not your typical journal.

This isn't about "fixing" you, improving your productivity, or turning you into some hyper-masculine ideal. This is a journal for the man who has carried too much, said too little, and felt unseen in the process. It's for the man who performs strength so well, no one notices when he's breaking inside.

Maybe that man is you.

UNHELD is a safe place — not to be perfect, but to be *present*. It's here to remind you that you are allowed to feel, to unravel, to be unsure, to rest, to breathe. You are allowed to want softness. You are allowed to want more.

Each page of this journal was written with you in mind. Not the version of you that holds it together for everyone else — but the one underneath. The one who aches for peace. The one who just wants to be heard.

You're not alone here. Welcome home to yourself.

Why This Journal Exists

For generations, men have been taught to hold it in.

We've inherited silences. We've worn masks so long they feel like skin. We've confused numbness for strength, isolation for pride, and exhaustion for worth. Somewhere along the way, we lost access to our full humanity — and with it, the tools to heal.

This journal was born from that ache.

UNHELD exists because men deserve a space to feel without judgment. To explore their minds and emotions without the burden of performance. To practice mindfulness in a way that is both powerful and practical. To unlearn, reframe, and reconnect.

It exists because silence is no longer sustainable — and your wholeness matters.

How to Use This Journal

You'll find **365 days** of intentional reflection — one for each day of your year. You can begin in January or July, on your birthday or after a breakdown. There's no wrong time to start showing up for yourself.

Each daily page includes:

A *Mindful Insight* to challenge, ground, or inspire you.

A *Prompt* to guide your reflection.

A *Mindful Minute* to pause and breathe.

An *Unheld Moment* — a truth, observation, or tension you may relate to.

Space to *journal freely* — for your thoughts, emotions, questions, or prayers.

At the end of each month, you'll find a **Monthly Reflection Page** to track your emotional growth, celebrate the unseen, and center your next steps.

You'll also have special pages for:

Letters You Never Sent — things you've always wanted to say.

Your Emotional Toolbox — practical coping tools and grounding techniques.

Daily Mantras — powerful affirmations for presence, softness, and strength.

Dreams, Goals & Visions — a space to imagine with no deadlines.

Coloring & Release Pages — spaces for creative expression and emotional release.

Use this journal daily, weekly, or whenever you need it. Let it be what it needs to be — some days a mirror, some days a friend.

What It Means to Be "Unheld"

To be **unheld** is to be strong in public and shattered in private.
It's the feeling of being praised for resilience no one helped you build.
It's knowing how to support others but not how to ask for support.
It's being so used to surviving, you forget what living feels like.

But this journal reclaims the word.

To be *unheld* here is not a flaw — it's a beginning.
It's the quiet truth that healing is overduc.
It's a man deciding that numbness is not his legacy.

This is not the end of you holding it together.
It's the beginning of you holding *yourself* — with grace.

Daily Reflection Structure

Every daily page in this journal is intentionally structured to support mindful masculinity — a balance of awareness, softness, and strength. Here's what to expect each day:

- **Mindful Insight**
  A daily observation, principle, or invitation rooted in mindfulness and emotional awareness.
- **Reflection Prompt**
  A thought-provoking question or prompt that encourages you to go inward and speak your truth.
- **Mindful Minute**
  A quick grounding practice — breathwork, stillness, gratitude, or presence. One minute is enough.
- **Unheld Moment**
  A relatable tension, truth, or struggle men carry but rarely name. You're not alone in this.
- **Daily Journaling Space**
  Blank space to write. No rules. Use it to vent, affirm, question, dream, or simply *be*.
- **Quarterly Progress Markers**
  At every 3-month interval, you'll pause for a deeper reflection — to honor your journey so far, reset your focus, and track your emotional evolution.

WEEK 1: THE INHERITED SILENCE

- **Theme:** Naming the silence passed down to you and the emotions buried beneath it.

- **Goal:** Begin unearthing emotional truths that were never allowed space.

DAY 1: The First Silence

There are different kinds of silence. Some are sacred— like the silence of awe, wonder, or peace. But others are heavy. The silence many men inherit is not calm but compressed. It's the silence of things that were too painful, too shameful, or too vulnerable to speak out loud. Fathers who never cried in front of us. Uncles who told us to "man up" when we were scared. Brothers who bottled everything up until it turned to anger.

That silence is passed down like an heirloom— generational, patterned, invisible but loud in its impact. And without realizing it, we've often continued the cycle: not speaking when we needed help, minimizing our own feelings, isolating ourselves because we thought that's what strength looked like.

But true strength begins with honesty. With naming what hurts. With reclaiming the words that were buried beneath expectations. Today, you don't have to say it all. But you can begin. You can whisper truth into the places that have long been quiet. That's how we heal—not only for ourselves, but for the boys watching us now.

Morning Reflection:

- **When did you first learn that your emotions made others uncomfortable?**

_____
_____
_____
_____
_____
_____
_____
_____

- **Was it in the face of your father's silence, or your mother's worry, or the world's unspoken rules?**

_____
_____
_____
_____
_____
_____

Prompt:

- **What emotion were you first taught to hide?**

_____
_____
_____
_____
_____
_____
_____
_____
_____
_____
_____
_____
_____
_____

Mindful Minute:

Sit still. Breathe in deeply. Say internally: *I was there. I remember.*

Breathe out: *But I am here now.*

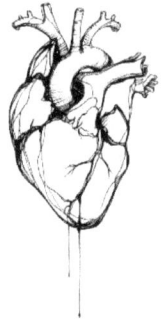

Mantra:

"I am allowed to feel what I was once told to fear."

Evening Reflection:

- What surfaced today — a memory, a feeling, or a silence — that deserves your attention? Can you name it without judgment?

_____
_____
_____
_____
_____
_____

Unheld Moment:

- You swallowed your feelings to keep the peace, but who kept yours?

Reflect on this

DAY 2: The Rules You Didn't Write

Masculinity, as we've known it, often teaches men that they must always be "on." Stoic. In control. The protector. The one who fixes things. The one who carries it all and never lets it show. Somewhere along the way, this became our armor. An identity we wear that gets mistaken for strength.

But armor is heavy. It restricts movement. It limits touch. And over time, it disconnects us from others—and ourselves. When your only mode is to be strong, there's no room to be real. You stop expressing pain. You downplay your joy. You become a version of yourself that is respected but not fully known.

True strength doesn't mean being emotionless. It means having the courage to be human. To say "I need help." To cry when it hurts. To laugh loudly when you feel joy. To tell the truth when it's hard.

You don't have to throw all the armor away today. But what's one piece you can set down, just for a while?

Morning Reflection:

- **Whose rules about manhood are you still following, even when they make you ache?**

_____
_____
_____
_____
_____
_____
_____
_____

Prompt:

- What "unwritten rules" about being a man shaped your boyhood?

_____
_____
_____
_____
_____
_____
_____
_____

Mindful Minute:

Stretch your arms wide. Say aloud: **I no longer shrink to fit their rules.**

Mantra:

"I am rewriting the story of what it means to be me."

Evening Reflection:

- **Did you notice a moment today when you acted out of habit — not truth?**

_____
_____
_____
_____
_____
_____
_____

Unheld Moment:

You weren't weak — you were adapting to survive.

DAY 3: The Cry You Never Let Out

You may not remember the first time you swallowed your pain, but your body does. Maybe you were told, "Man up," or, "Stop crying like a girl." Or maybe you were met with silence—your sadness left hanging in the air, unheld. Over time, you learned to retreat into yourself. To harden. To perform okay-ness even when you were unraveling.

But grief has a way of lingering. It shows up in other places: irritability, distance, distraction, even physical tension. That cry you never let out didn't disappear—it just changed forms.

Men have been taught to grieve in silence, to mourn in private, if at all. But what if we made space to weep—not just for the things we lost, but for the selves we abandoned to survive?

It's okay to be the man who cries. Who grieves. Who cracks open the door to healing by releasing what's been buried.

Morning Reflection:

Tears don't make you fragile. They are a language of honesty.

Prompt:

- Recall a moment when you needed to cry but didn't. What stopped you?

_____
_____
_____
_____
_____
_____
_____
_____

Mindful Minute:

Close your eyes. Place a hand on your chest. Whisper: *I give myself permission.*

Mantra:

"What I hold in my body, I can also let go."

Evening Reflection:

Was there a small release today — a breath, a tear, a memory unburied? Honor it. It matters.

Unheld Moment:

That lump in your throat — it was a dam, not weakness.

DAY 4: The Lessons of Quiet Fathers

Some men are raised by fathers who rarely speak of emotions—who express love through acts of provision or presence, but not always in words. Maybe your father was a provider, stoic and dutiful. Or maybe he was absent—emotionally or physically—and that silence left you to fill in the blanks.

What we don't hear, we often internalize. You may have learned that love is duty, not affection. That presence is enough, even when the heart is missing from the room. That silence is strength—even when it's loneliness dressed as discipline.

But quiet fathers aren't just puzzles to decode—they're mirrors. Their silence teaches us what we might withhold. Their emotional absence becomes the invitation to show up differently.

You don't have to become what he couldn't express. You get to rewrite the emotional legacy.

Morning Reflection:

Sometimes the loudest lessons come from the ones who never spoke them.

Prompt:

- **What did your father — or the men who raised you — teach you through their silence?**

_____
_____
_____
_____
_____
_____
_____

Mindful Minute:

Lightly tap your chest with your fingertips. Let your body remember that you're allowed to speak.

Mantra:

"I break cycles by naming what they never said."

Evening Reflection:

- **What would you say to the boy who needed more?**

_____
_____
_____
_____
_____
_____
_____
_____

Unheld Moment:

You made silence your language because no one offered you another.

DAY 5: Protectors Who Were Also Hurting

Many of the men we looked up to were protectors—strong, present, and seemingly unshakable. But strength can sometimes be armor, and protection can mask deep pain.
Fathers, uncles, brothers, and mentors who shielded us from the world often never learned how to shield themselves from their own wounds.

They bore their burdens quietly. Maybe they worked long hours, never complained, stayed composed in chaos. But if you looked closely, their exhaustion showed. Their silence had weight. Their anger had roots.

We honor our protectors by seeing the full truth: they were brave, and they were breaking. They gave what they had, even if it wasn't everything we needed. This acknowledgment doesn't diminish their strength—it humanizes it.

You are allowed to be a protector and still hurt. You are allowed to protect yourself, too.

Morning Reflection:

What if the men who shaped you were never shown how to be whole?

Prompt:

- **Think of a male figure from your childhood. What might he have been carrying?**

_____
_____
_____
_____
_____
_____
_____
_____

Mindful Minute:

Offer this breath to those who couldn't show up — and to yourself, who still needed them.

Mantra:

"I carry pain, but I do not have to pass it on."

Evening Reflection:

- **Did compassion shift your anger today — or deepen your grief?**

Both are valid.

Unheld Moment:

You inherited pain from people who never got to heal.

DAY 6: When You Disappeared to Belong

There are versions of yourself that you abandoned—not because you wanted to, but because you thought you had to. Maybe you learned to shrink your softness, mute your passions, or bury your truth just to fit in. Maybe your survival depended on it—on being accepted, unthreatening, or invulnerable.

Masculinity, in its most rigid form, often demands disappearance. It tells boys to toughen up, stop crying, push through, and don't ask for help. So we disappear—emotionally, spiritually, even creatively—to earn belonging in spaces that punish authenticity.

But your belonging should never cost you your wholeness.

If you've ever lost yourself trying to be enough for others, know this: you're allowed to come back. You're allowed to reclaim the parts of you that were left behind. You're allowed to belong to yourself again.

Morning Reflection:

You didn't lose yourself — you hid yourself to stay accepted.

Prompt:

- **When did you first realize that being yourself might cost you belonging?**

_____
_____
_____
_____
_____
_____
_____

Mindful Minute:

Stand in front of a mirror. Make eye contact. Say: *I still see you. I still choose you.*

Mantra:

"The parts I hid to survive are now safe with me."

Evening Reflection:

- **What did you reclaim today — a word, a truth, a presence?**

_____
_____
_____
_____
_____
_____
_____
_____

Unheld Moment:

You were told to "man up" — but no one taught you what that actually meant.

DAY 7: You're not Broken — You're Unlearning

You are not broken. You are not too much. You are not behind. What you are is *in process*—unlearning what never belonged to you in the first place.

For years, you were conditioned to believe that silence was strength, detachment was discipline, and suppression was maturity. So when your emotions rose like tides or your heart longed for connection, you were taught to shame it, hide it, deny it. Now, as you begin to reclaim your truth, it can feel messy, confusing—even painful. But that doesn't mean you're failing.

It means you're healing.

Unlearning is sacred work. It is the slow peeling back of stories that hardened you. It is the gentle reintroduction to softness, to honesty, to breath. It takes courage. It takes repetition. But most of all, it takes compassion—for yourself.

You don't need fixing. You need space. Space to grieve the roles you performed. Space to remember who you were before the world told you who to be.

You are not broken. You are returning.

Morning Reflection:

There's nothing wrong with you. There's only what you were taught — and what you are now choosing.

Prompt:

- **What belief about yourself are you ready to unlearn?**

_____
_____
_____
_____
_____
_____
_____
_____

Mindful Minute:

Breathe in: *I forgive myself for forgetting who I am.*
Breathe out: *I remember now.*

Mantra:

"Healing isn't becoming someone new — it's coming back to myself."

Evening Reflection:

- **Where did you catch yourself today — in thought, in speech, in silence — and choose differently?**

_____
_____
_____
_____
_____
_____

Unheld Moment:

You mistook survival for identity. But you are more than what you've endured.

WEEK 2: MASCULINITY ISN'T A COSTUME

Theme: Peeling off the performance of "being a man" to discover your honest self.

Goal: Examine the pressures of performative masculinity and create room for authenticity.

DAY 8: The Masks We Wear

From an early age, many men are taught to wear masks— crafted from toughness, silence, control, or perfection.
These masks become survival tools: to hide vulnerability, to gain approval, to protect the parts of you that never felt safe being seen.

But with time, the mask becomes heavy. The smile you wear when you're exhausted. The "I'm fine" you say when your soul is unraveling. The roles you perform just to fit into rooms that don't feel like home. It's no wonder so many men feel unknown—even to themselves.

What happens when the mask comes off?

At first, it may feel like exposure. But with it comes relief. The breath you've been holding. The tears you've postponed. The laughter that's real. The life that's yours.

This isn't about abandoning strength. It's about broadening the definition. Strength includes softness, honesty, and asking for help. It includes showing up authentically—even when your voice shakes.

You deserve a life that doesn't require you to pretend.

Morning Reflection:

- What parts of you feel like a performance — even in your quietest moments?

_____
_____
_____
_____
_____
_____
_____
_____

Prompt:

- **When did you first feel that you had to "act like a man"?**

_____
_____
_____
_____
_____
_____
_____
_____
_____

Mindful Minute:

Inhale: *I no longer have to perform.*

Exhale: *I am safe to be real.*

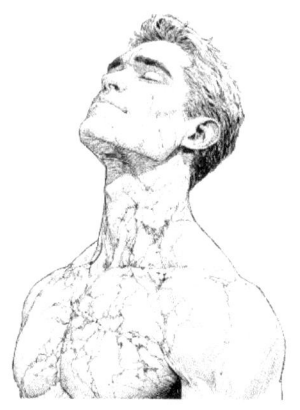

Mantra:

"I don't have to pretend to be strong. I already am."

Evening Reflection:

- Did you notice a moment today where you softened instead of performing?

_____
_____
_____
_____
_____
_____
_____

- **What did it feel like?**

_____
_____
_____
_____
_____
_____
_____
_____

Unheld Moment:

Being honest about your needs isn't weakness — it's clarity.

DAY 9: The Weight of Expectations

Before you had a chance to define yourself, the world handed you a script: Be the strong one. Be the provider. Be the one who doesn't cry. Be everything to everyone—but never a burden to anyone.

The expectations placed on men often go unseen because they've been normalized. You're expected to carry pain in silence, make sacrifices without complaint, and keep moving even when you're running on empty. And when you struggle, you're told to "man up," as if humanity is something to suppress.

These invisible weights don't just exhaust the body—they distort identity. You begin to measure your worth by how well you perform rather than how deeply you feel. You learn to hide your needs so others don't feel uncomfortable. You shrink your truth to fit into a mold that never really felt right.

But here's the truth: You are not weak for feeling tired. You are not failing because you want softness, connection, or space to just be. You are not alone for questioning the rules.

Unlearning begins with acknowledging the weight. And healing begins with the choice to set some of it down.

You were never meant to carry it all.

Morning Reflection:

Masculinity isn't one-size-fits-all — but the world often acts like it is.

Prompt:

- **What expectations have been placed on your shoulders because you're a man?**

_____
_____
_____
_____
_____
_____
_____

Mindful Minute:

Close your eyes. With every exhale, imagine setting down one invisible weight.

Mantra:

"My worth is not defined by how much I carry."

Evening Reflection:

- **What pressure did you notice yourself pushing against today?**

_____
_____
_____
_____
_____
_____
_____
_____

Unheld Moment:

You don't have to prove your manhood — just live your truth.

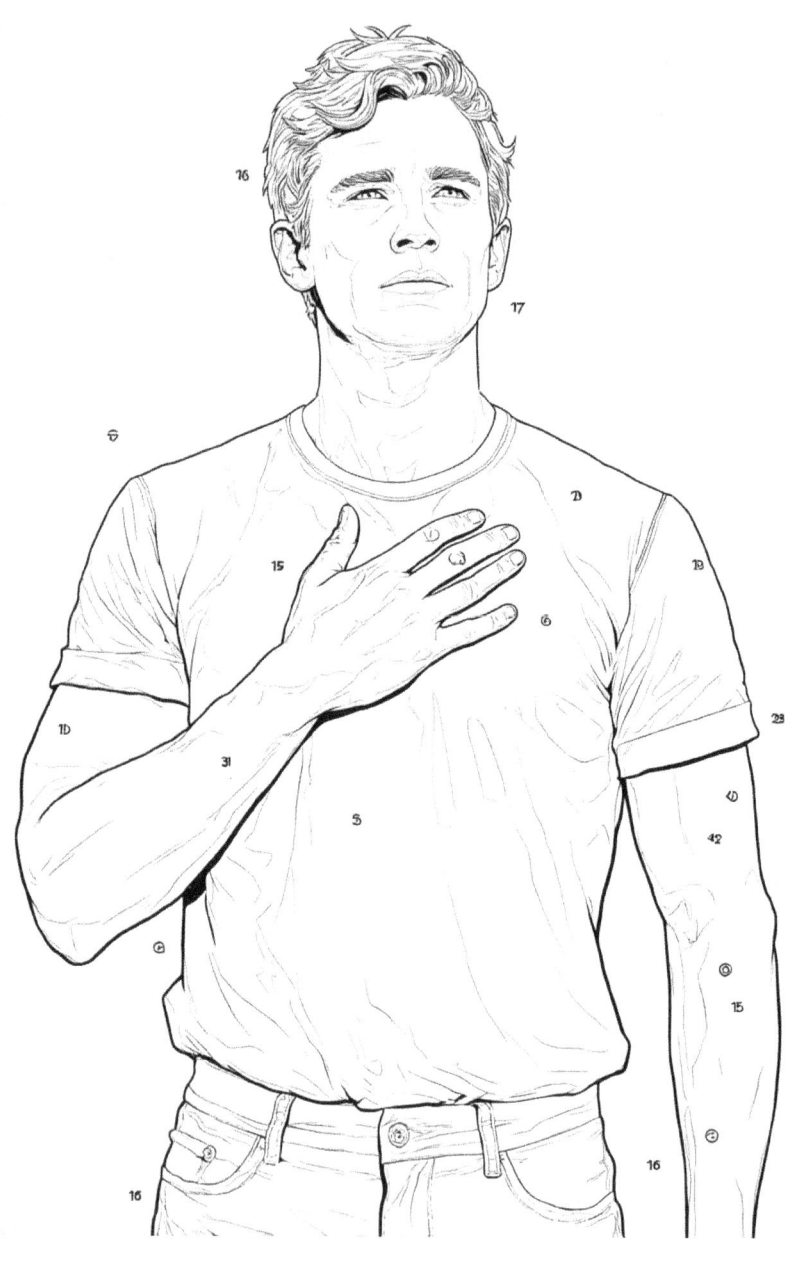

Day 10: Strength Isn't Stoicism

Strength was never supposed to mean silence. But somewhere along the line, many men were taught that to be strong is to endure alone—to bury pain, to never flinch, to always have it together.

You became the one others leaned on. The fixer. The solid ground. And maybe you're proud of that. Maybe being dependable gave you purpose. But over time, that strength began to cost you: your needs, your softness, your voice.

No one asks how you're doing because you've trained them not to. You downplay your own struggles so others won't worry. And when you do speak up, it feels like betrayal—to the image of the strong man you've carefully maintained.

But real strength doesn't live in hiding.

Real strength is the courage to say, "I'm not okay." It's the wisdom to ask for help, the integrity to tell the truth, the softness to feel, and the power to stop pretending.

You are allowed to rest. You are allowed to receive. And you are allowed to be fully human.

Being strong should never cost you your wholeness.

Mindful Minute:

Place both hands over your heart. Breathe deeply.

Repeat silently: *I give my strength a softer name.*

Morning Reflection:

What if real strength is your ability to be soft?

Prompt:

- **Who told you that showing emotions was weak?**

_____
_____
_____
_____
_____
_____
_____

Mantra:

"I can cry and still be powerful."

Evening Reflection:

- Did you let yourself feel something uncomfortable today without numbing it?

Reflect on this.

Unheld Moment:

You were never meant to be a statue. You were built to feel.

DAY 11: The Performance of Power

Power, for many men, was never just about influence — it was survival. From a young age, you may have learned that showing power meant earning respect. That commanding space meant safety. That controlling your emotions meant control over your world.

But much of what you've called power was performance — armor worn to hide the ache, the fear, the tender questions beneath. You puffed your chest when you felt unseen. You spoke louder when you felt unheard. You acted certain when doubt quietly gnawed at you.

This performance often won applause, promotions, and proximity to influence — but it may have cost you authenticity, connection, and rest.

You are not less of a man when you stop performing.

True power is quiet, grounded, and clear. It doesn't demand, it invites. It doesn't pretend, it reveals. And it doesn't dominate, it liberates — starting with the self.

Today, lay down the mask of control. Let your presence, not performance, speak for you.

Prompt:

- **When do you use control to feel safe?**

_____
_____
_____
_____
_____
_____
_____

Mindful Minute:

Breathe in: *I release the need to control.*

Breathe out: *I trust myself to respond.*

Mantra:

"Letting go is not the same as losing."

Evening Reflection:

- **Where did you try to manage too much today?**

_____
_____
_____
_____
_____
_____
_____

- **What would it look like to ask for help next time?**

_____
_____
_____
_____
_____
_____
_____
_____

Unheld Moment:

Power rooted in fear can't protect what matters most.

DAY 12: Letting the Real You Breathe

You've spent years adjusting—fitting into molds, reading rooms, withholding parts of yourself to be accepted, respected, or simply left alone. Somewhere along the way, the *real* you—the quiet hopes, the quirky joys, the unfiltered feelings—got buried under layers of what felt necessary.

But the you that you hide still longs to be seen. Not for performance. Not for perfection. But for presence.

Letting the real you breathe is not a collapse of everything you've built—it's a gentle homecoming. One honest laugh. One true no. One yes that feels like freedom.

Start small. Let something unpolished show. Let someone in a little more. Not everyone deserves access, but *you* deserve expression.

Today, loosen the grip. Let one part of you that's been holding its breath... exhale.

Morning Reflection:

There's a version of you beneath the layers — soft, honest, human.

Prompt:

- **If you weren't performing or protecting, what would your day look like?**

_____
_____
_____
_____
_____
_____
_____
_____

Mindful Minute:

Stretch your shoulders. Roll your neck gently.

Say out loud: *This is my body. It doesn't have to armor up today.*

Mantra:

"I am enough when I'm not hiding."

Evening Reflection:

- **What felt honest today?**

_____
_____
_____
_____
_____
_____
_____
_____

- **What part of you got to breathe?**

_____
_____
_____
_____
_____
_____
_____
_____

Unheld Moment:

You're not too much — and you never were.

DAY 13: Defining Manhood for Yourself

For too long, "manhood" has been defined by voices that didn't know your story, your tenderness, or your truth. You were handed a script—be hard, don't cry, always provide, never fall. And yet, somewhere deep down, you've always known: that's not the full story.

Real manhood isn't one-size-fits-all. It's not confined to how much you earn, how quiet you stay, or how much pain you carry without showing it.

It's defined by your integrity. Your capacity to care. Your courage to heal. Your ability to stand fully in your truth—even when it doesn't match the world's outdated definitions.

Today, take one step toward the version of manhood that feels true to you. Not what you were told to be—but who you're becoming, with honesty, softness, and strength combined.

Morning Reflection:

If manhood had no definition — no rules — what would it mean to you?

Prompt:

- **What does healthy masculinity look and feel like to *you*? (Not the world. Not your father. You.)**

_____
_____
_____
_____
_____
_____
_____
_____

Mindful Minute:

Place both hands on your chest and say:

I define who I am. I define my masculinity.

Mantra:

"My manhood is mine to define — not inherit."

Evening Reflection:

- **Did you catch yourself today acting out of someone else's definition of manhood?**

_____
_____
_____
_____
_____
_____
_____
_____

- How would you rewrite that script?

_____
_____
_____
_____
_____
_____
_____
_____

Unheld Moment:

You don't have to fit into their blueprint — you're allowed to build your own.

DAY 14: Coming Home to Yourself

There's a kind of exhaustion that doesn't come from doing too much—it comes from being too far from yourself for too long.

You've spent years showing up as who you were expected to be. Fitting in. Providing. Protecting. Performing. But what about *being*? What about the version of you that doesn't have to try so hard?

Coming home to yourself is an act of courage. It's peeling off the layers placed on you by culture, family, survival. It's remembering who you were before the world told you who to be.

This isn't about arriving at perfection—it's about returning to presence. It's about sitting with your emotions, reclaiming your voice, trusting your pace.

You deserve a life that feels like yours. Not just in moments of solitude—but in the way you move through the world, unapologetically and whole.

Morning Reflection:

Every day you unlearn a lie is a day you return to your true self.

Prompt:

- **What's something you no longer believe about what it means to be a man?**

_____
_____
_____
_____
_____
_____
_____
_____

Mindful Minute:

Inhale through your nose. Exhale through your mouth. Repeat three times: *I'm not broken — I'm becoming.*

Mantra:

"The man I'm becoming is the boy I once needed."

Evening Reflection:

- How did you honor the boy in you today — the one who only wanted to be seen?

_____
_____
_____
_____
_____
_____
_____
_____

Unheld Moment:

This journey back to yourself is the most courageous thing you've ever done.

WEEK 3: STRONG BUT NUMB

Theme: Strength without vulnerability is emotional isolation.
Goal: Begin reconnecting with your feelings by safely identifying and naming them.

You've worn strength like armor — but beneath it, you've gone quiet.
This week is about tuning back in.

Not to weakness, but to truth.
Not to overwhelm, but to wholeness.

You'll begin feeling again — slowly, safely, without shame.
Numbness helped you survive. But now, you're ready to live.

DAY 15: Numb Isn't Neutral

Numbness often wears the disguise of strength. But let's be honest—numb isn't peace. It isn't calm. And it sure isn't neutral.

When you turn off pain, you turn off joy. When you silence grief, you muffle laughter. And while it might feel easier in the moment to disconnect, over time, that silence starts to cost you parts of yourself.

Numbness is a response to too much—too much hurt, too much pressure, too little room to feel. But healing asks you to feel again, even when it's uncomfortable.

You don't have to dive headfirst into the emotions you've locked away. But you can begin, gently. Pay attention to what makes you blink twice. What tugs at your chest. What softens your jaw.

You are not a machine. You are a human being. And being fully alive means making space for the whole spectrum—not just the parts you've been taught are acceptable.

Morning Reflection:

Numbness is not nothingness. It's a wall your body built to survive.

Prompt:

What emotions have you silenced so long that now they feel... gone?

_____
_____
_____
_____
_____
_____

Mindful Minute:

Place one hand on your chest and whisper: *"I give myself permission to feel again."*

Mantra:

"Numbness is a signal — not a failure."

Evening Reflection:

- **Did you feel disconnected today? What do you think your numbness might be protecting you from?**

_____
_____
_____
_____
_____
_____
_____

Unheld Moment:

You don't need to judge your emotional silence. Just notice it.

DAY 16: Where Does It Hurt?

Pause for a moment. Scan your body, your heart, your memory.

Where does it hurt?

Not just physically, but emotionally. Mentally. Spiritually.

It's a question we rarely ask ourselves. We power through the days. We perform. We protect. But we often forget to check in with the person behind it all—ourselves.

That tension in your chest, the lump in your throat, the ache in your back—it might be telling a story your mouth hasn't dared to speak. It might be grief. Or disappointment. Or the weight of everything you've been carrying alone.

Naming the pain doesn't make you weak. It makes you honest. And honesty is the beginning of healing.

So today, ask yourself—where does it hurt? And then give yourself permission to listen.

Morning Reflection:

Emotional pain doesn't disappear — it just changes form.

Prompt:

- If your emotional pain had a voice or location in your body, what would it say? Where would it live?

_____
_____
_____
_____
_____
_____
_____
_____
_____
_____
_____
_____

Mindful Minute:

- **Close your eyes. Scan your body from head to toe. Where are you holding pain?**

_____
_____
_____
_____
_____
_____
_____
_____
_____
_____
_____
_____
_____

Mantra:

"I carry pain, but it does not carry me."

Evening Reflection:

- Was there a moment you noticed tension today? Did you explore it or ignore it?

_____
_____
_____
_____
_____
_____
_____
_____
_____
_____

Unheld Moment:

Your body remembers what your mind tries to forget.

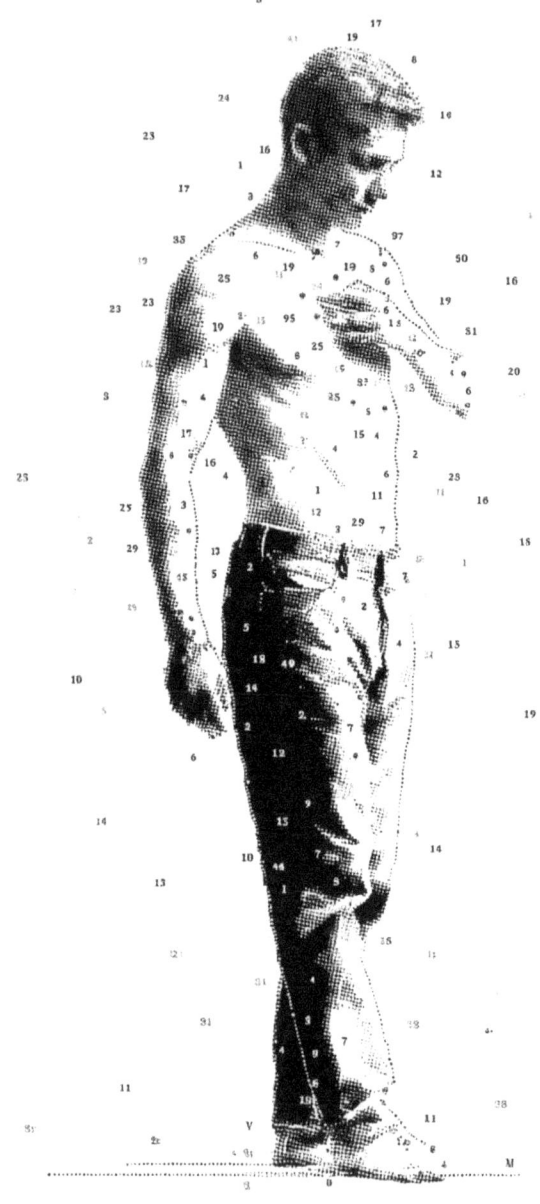

DAY 17: Feelings Aren't Facts — But They Matter

Your feelings may not always be accurate representations of reality—but they are real.

They carry truth, not always in what they *say*, but in *why* they show up. Fear might exaggerate the danger, but it signals that you feel unsafe. Sadness might not mean you've failed, but it reveals a longing or loss.

As men, we're taught to dismiss feelings as irrational, dramatic, or even dangerous. But ignoring emotions doesn't make us strong—it makes us disconnected.

You don't need to act on every feeling, but you do need to acknowledge them. They're messengers. They tell you what matters, what hurts, what needs attention.

So today, resist the urge to argue with your emotions. Instead, get curious:
What is this feeling trying to reveal?

Morning Reflection:

You don't have to *be* your emotions — just feel them.

Prompt:

- **What are 3 feelings you've been told are "too much"? Who told you that?**

_____
_____
_____
_____
_____
_____
_____
_____
_____

Mindful Minute:

Breathe in: *"My emotions are visitors."*

Breathe out: *"I can greet them without fear."*

Mantra:

"I feel — and that's a sign I'm alive."

Evening Reflection:

- **What emotion visited today? Did you notice how your body responded to it?**

_____
_____
_____
_____
_____
_____
_____
_____

Unheld Moment:

You can survive your emotions without suppressing them.

DAY 18: You Can Be Both

You can be soft and strong.
You can be disciplined and tender.
You can lead and still ask for help.

Masculinity has often been painted in extremes—either stoic or emotionally messy, either powerful or passive. But real wholeness exists in the *and*.

You can grieve and keep going.
You can hold space for others and still need your own.
You can be healing and not yet healed.

This isn't about choosing one part of you over another. It's about integration.

Let yourself be both. It's not a contradiction—it's a fuller version of your truth.

Morning Reflection:

You can be strong and struggling. You can be a provider and still need support.

Prompt:

- **Where in your life do you force yourself to be "the strong one"?**

_____
_____
_____
_____
_____
_____
_____
_____
_____

- **What would it cost to admit you're tired?**

_____
_____
_____
_____
_____
_____
_____
_____

Mindful Minute:

Place your palm over your heart. Say: *"I honor the tension inside me."*

Mantra:

"I am not either/or — I am both/and."

Evening Reflection:

- **Did you notice any contradictions within yourself today?**

_____
_____
_____
_____
_____
_____
_____
_____
_____
_____

Unheld Moment:

You don't have to choose between power and tenderness.

DAY 19: The Quiet Cost of Numbing

Numbing doesn't always look like painkillers or liquor.
Sometimes, it looks like workaholism.
Scrolling.
Silence.
Busyness.
Laughter that doesn't reach your eyes.

We often numb not because we're weak—but because we've learned it's unsafe to feel.
But numbness isn't neutral. It costs you your connection to joy, to clarity, to the parts of yourself still waiting to be witnessed.

You don't need to feel everything all at once.
You just need to *start* feeling again—bit by bit.

The cost of numbing is your aliveness.
And you deserve to feel fully alive.

Morning Reflection:

When you numb pain, you often numb joy too.

Prompt:

- What beautiful moments have you missed by shutting down your emotions?

_____
_____
_____
_____
_____
_____
_____
_____

Mindful Minute:

Hold something cold (ice, chilled glass). Notice the sensation fully.

That's what feeling *fully* can be like — sharp but real.

Mantra:

"I want my life in full color — not grayscale."

Evening Reflection:

- **Did you let yourself fully enjoy or feel something today? What got in the way?**

_____
_____
_____
_____
_____
_____
_____
_____

Unheld Moment:

Joy is a risk worth taking — even if you're not used to it.

DAY 20: Emotional Muscles

Just like physical muscles, your emotional muscles grow with intentional use.
You don't expect to bench press 200 pounds on your first try—so why expect yourself to process years of buried emotions overnight?

Emotional strength isn't about suppression or stoicism. It's about facing discomfort, staying with what's true, and building your capacity to hold it with grace.
Tears don't make you weak. Vulnerability isn't collapse.

Every time you name what you feel, you're doing reps. Every time you speak up instead of shutting down, you're getting stronger.

Keep going.
You're not failing—you're in training.

Morning Reflection:

Naming emotions is a skill — not something you're supposed to "just know."

Prompts:

Pick three emotions from today. Now go deeper: What triggered them?

_____
_____
_____
_____
_____
_____
_____
_____
_____

- **What did they want you to notice?**

_____
_____
_____
_____
_____
_____
_____

Mindful Minute:

Take a deep breath and whisper: *"I am learning my emotional language, one word at a time."*

Mantra:

"Feelings are signals, not threats."

Evening Reflection:

- **Were you able to name a feeling today instead of reacting to it?**

_____
_____
_____
_____
_____
_____
_____
_____
_____

Unheld Moment:

You're not broken for needing practice. You're building strength.

DAY 21: The Truth Underneath

What you think is anger might actually be grief.
What you label as laziness might be exhaustion.
Sometimes, silence is shame in disguise.

Men are often taught to name the surface—"I'm fine," "I'm pissed," "I'm tired"—
but rarely invited to look underneath.

The truth is softer, more vulnerable.
It doesn't always sound strong, but it's *real*.
And in that realness is your strength.

Don't stop at the surface.
Ask yourself: *"What's actually here?"*
The more honest you are with yourself, the freer you become.

Morning Reflection:

Anger is often a cover. What's underneath it?

Prompt:

- When was the last time you got angry?

_____
_____
_____
_____
_____
_____
_____

- Beneath the surface, what were you really feeling?

_____
_____
_____
_____
_____
_____
_____

Mindful Minute:

Inhale deeply. As you exhale, ask: *"What am I really trying to protect?"*

Mantra:

"Behind my anger lives a softer truth."

Evening Reflection:

- **Did anger show up today?**

_____
_____
_____
_____
_____
_____
_____
_____

- **What did it teach you about your real needs?**

_____
_____
_____
_____
_____
_____
_____
_____

Unheld Moment:

You don't need to fight to be heard. You just need to listen to yourself first.

WEEK 4: THE PRESSURE OF PROVIDING

This week confronts the invisible load many men carry — the deep-rooted belief that our worth is measured by how much we provide, produce, or endure. We begin to untangle the difference between contribution and identity. You are more than your utility.

Day 22: The Provider Script

You were likely taught that to be a man means to provide.
To bring the money.
To meet the needs.
To never lack.

But somewhere along the line, that script stopped making room for *you*.
It stopped asking how *you're* doing.
It didn't care about your dreams, your rest, your peace—only your output.

Providing is noble.
But when it becomes your identity, it can bury your humanity.
You're more than what you can give.

It's okay to want a life that also feeds *you*.
It's okay to rewrite the script.

Morning Reflection:

What messages did you inherit about being a provider? Did they come with love — or with fear?

Prompt:

- **What do I believe providing looks like?**

_____
_____
_____
_____
_____
_____
_____

Mindful Minute:

Close your eyes. Breathe in deeply, allowing your chest to expand without tension. Say inwardly, "I am enough."

Breathe out slowly and let go of any pressure to prove your value today.

Mantra:

"I offer more than provision — I offer presence."

Evening Reflection:

- When today did I equate my worth with output? What would I say to my younger self about being "enough"?

_____
_____
_____
_____
_____
_____
_____

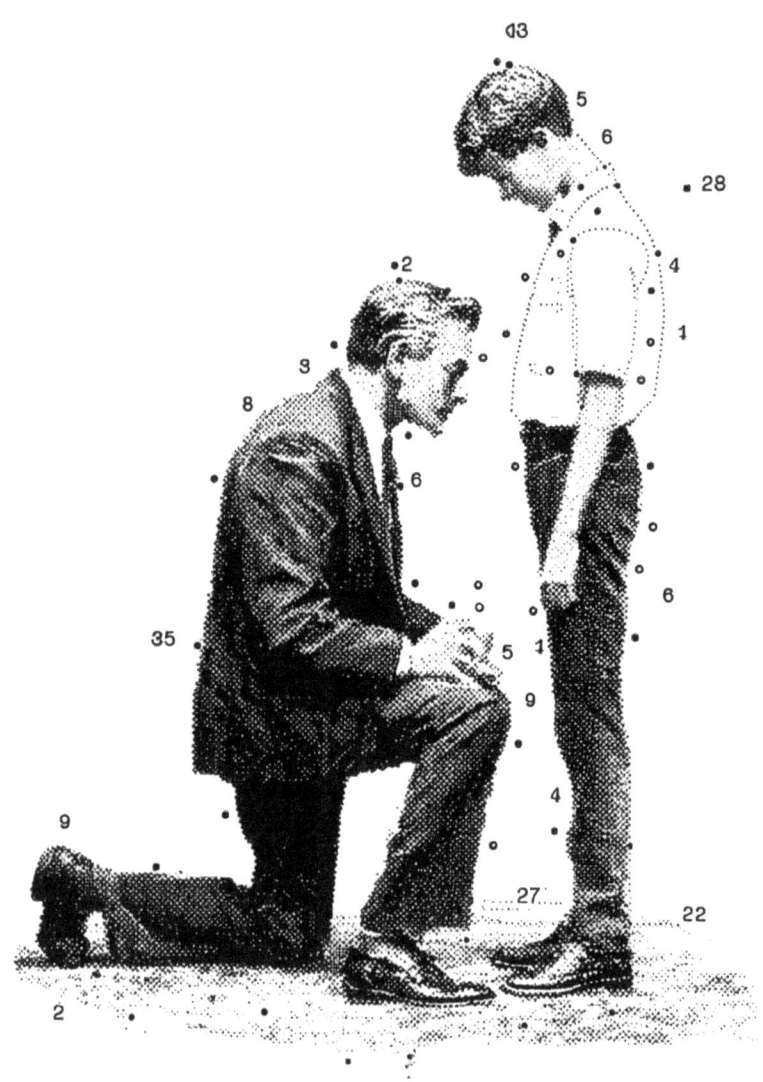

Day 23: Contribution without Exhaustion

You want your life to mean something.
You want to contribute—to your family, your work, your people.
That desire is sacred.

But somewhere along the line, you were taught that contribution must come through depletion.
That being needed is more important than being well.

You don't have to prove your worth through overextension.
You don't have to break your back to be valuable.

Let your contribution come from overflow, not emptiness.
Give what you have *without losing yourself in the giving.*

Morning Reflection:

You can give without draining. The goal is contribution, not depletion.

Prompt:

- **Where am I overextending myself out of guilt or obligation?**

_____
_____
_____
_____
_____
_____
_____

Mindful Minute:

Sit quietly with your hands relaxed. With each breath, scan your body for tension. Visualize your energy refilling — not draining.

Mantra:

"I can contribute from a full cup."

Evening Reflection:

- Did I give more than I had to give today?

_____
_____
_____
_____
_____
_____

- Where could I have paused or asked for support?

_____
_____
_____
_____
_____
_____
_____

Day 24: Unspoken Pressure

No one had to say it out loud.
You felt it in the glances, the silence, the expectations.
Be strong. Be steady. Don't break.

It's the kind of pressure that creeps in quietly—
Not from enemies, but from people who love you.

You learned to smile through the struggle.
To carry weight without complaint.
To succeed, even if it cost you sleep, peace, or authenticity.

But pressure isn't love.
And silence isn't strength.

You're allowed to acknowledge the weight.
You're allowed to ask for help.
You don't have to keep proving what you've already survived.

Morning Reflection:

- Unspoken expectations can feel heavier than spoken ones.

- Whose voice are you trying to please in your mind?

Reflect on these.

Prompt:

- What pressure am I carrying that was never clearly asked of me — but I still feel?

_____
_____
_____
_____
_____
_____
_____
_____

Mindful Minute:

Imagine setting down a backpack of invisible bricks — each one labeled with someone else's expectation. Let your shoulders drop.

Mantra:

"I release what was never mine to carry."

Evening Reflection:

- What expectation felt loudest today? Was it mine, or someone else's?

_____
_____
_____
_____
_____
_____
_____

Day 25 – The Lie of Self-Sacrifice

You were taught that love looks like sacrifice—
That being a good man means giving until there's nothing left.
But martyrdom is not masculinity.

Yes, love requires effort.
But not erasure.

You don't have to disappear to be good.
You don't have to be exhausted to be enough.
You don't have to suffer to be seen as strong.

Your needs matter.
Your joy matters.
And when you care for yourself,
You teach others how to care for you too.

Morning Reflection:

Sacrifice isn't always noble when it silences your needs.

Prompt:

- Where have I made myself small to meet others' needs?

_____
_____
_____
_____
_____
_____
_____

Mindful Minute:

Place one hand on your chest. Say softly, "I matter too."

Mantra:

"Honoring myself is not selfish."

Evening Reflection:

- Did I acknowledge my own needs today, or did I push them aside?

_____
_____
_____
_____
_____
_____
_____

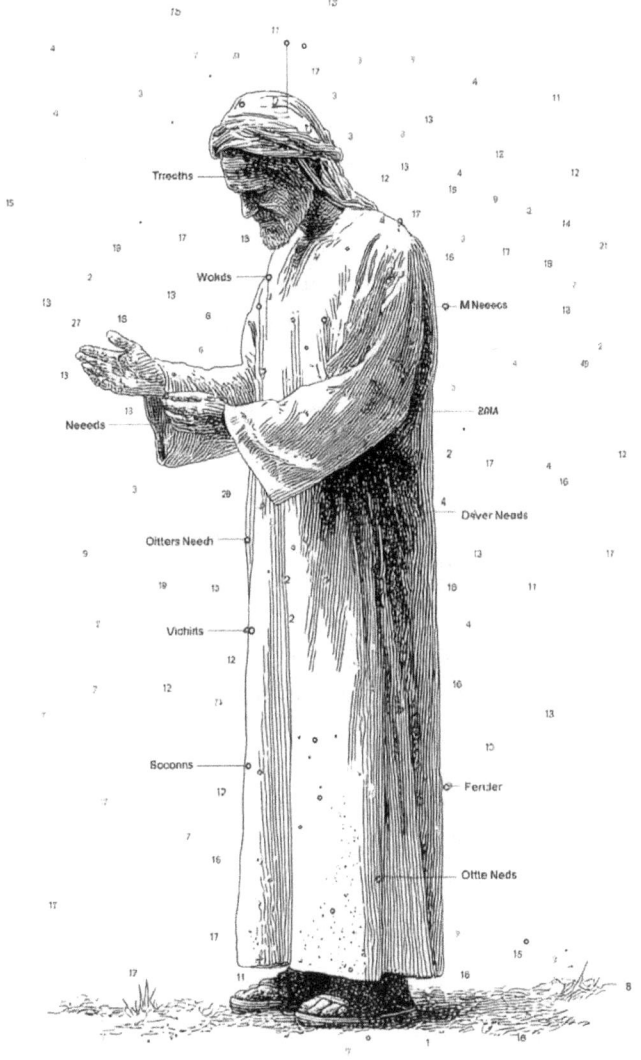

Day 26: Redefining Strength

Strength was once silence.
Swallowing pain. Bearing it alone.
But real strength doesn't look like pretending.

It looks like honesty.
Like asking for help when you need it.
Like telling the truth even when your voice shakes.

It's not about how much you can carry—
It's about how willing you are to put something down when it's breaking you.

Strength is showing up—fully.
Even when it's messy.
Even when it's vulnerable.
Even when the world told you to hide.

Morning Reflection:

Being strong doesn't mean never needing help. Strength is asking, too.

Prompt:

- **What keeps me from reaching out or asking for support?**

_____
_____
_____
_____
_____
_____
_____

Mindful Minute:

Close your eyes. Imagine a circle of people you trust — offering help, not judgment. Breathe that in.

Mantra:

"Strength welcomes support."

Evening Reflection:

- **Was there a moment I could have asked for help today but didn't?**

_____
_____
_____
_____
_____
_____
_____
_____

- **Why?**

_____
_____
_____
_____
_____
_____
_____
_____

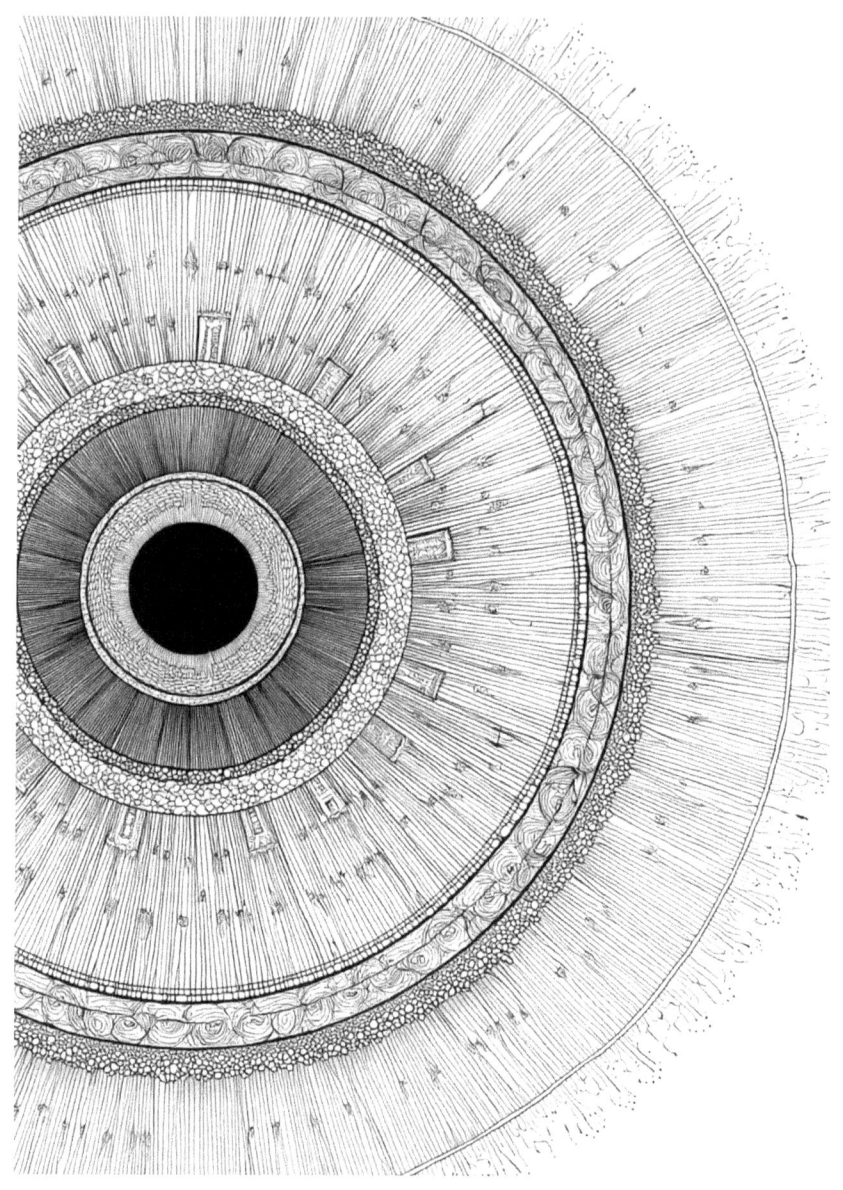

Day 27: The Value of Being, Not Doing

You were raised to prove your worth through productivity.
To earn love by what you accomplish.
To be seen only when you're useful.

But who are you when you're not fixing, achieving, or striving?
You still matter.

Your value isn't in what you do—
It's in who you are.
Your breath is enough. Your presence is enough.
You are worthy, even in stillness.

Let yourself be.
Without a goal.
Without a role.
Just be.

Morning Reflection:

You don't have to earn rest. You are valuable even in stillness.

Prompt:

- **How do I feel when I'm not "doing" anything?**

_____
_____
_____
_____
_____
_____
_____

- **What story does that tell me?**

_____
_____
_____
_____
_____
_____
_____
_____

Mindful Minute:

Sit still and notice five sensations without labeling or judging. Just be.

Mantra:

"My being is enough."

Evening Reflection:

- **Did I give myself permission to rest or slow down today? How did it feel?**

_____
_____
_____
_____
_____
_____
_____
_____

Day 28: Choosing Wholeness Over Performance

You learned to perform for love—
To say the right things, wear the right mask,
Be the strong one, the funny one, the silent one.

But the applause never healed the ache.
Because performance can't replace presence.
And pretending robs you of being known.

Wholeness asks for honesty.
It invites the parts of you you've hidden:
The tender, the tired, the terrified.

You don't have to impress anyone today.
Just choose to be real.
Wholeness is where your healing begins.

Morning Reflection:

You're not here to perform a version of yourself for applause. You're here to live as your whole self.

Prompt:

- **Where in my life do I perform instead of just being honest?**

_____
_____
_____
_____
_____
_____
_____
_____

Mindful Minute:

Inhale deeply and say, "I am safe to be real." Exhale tension and any masks you've worn.

Mantra:

"I choose wholeness over performance."

Evening Reflection:

- **Did I show up honestly today — even if it felt imperfect?**

_____
_____
_____
_____
_____
_____
_____
_____
_____
_____

Month 1 Reflection: Self-Awareness Begins

1. **A Letter to Self**

- **Write to yourself. Offer grace. Set your tone for the journey ahead.**

_____
_____
_____
_____
_____
_____
_____
_____

WEEK 5: INVISIBLE BURDENS

Not all weight is physical. This week explores the quiet loads you carry — the mental strain, emotional armor, and responsibilities that often go unnoticed. Naming your burdens is the first step in loosening their grip.

Day 29: The Things I Don't Say

There are words lodged in the back of your throat,
sentences edited before they ever reach your lips.

You learned early that silence was safer—
that speaking your need might make you a burden.
So you nod, smile, shift the focus,
and hold your ache like it's a secret only you can carry.

But holding it in doesn't make it smaller.
Swallowing pain doesn't make you stronger.

Some truths don't need to be loud—
they just need to be heard,
even if it's only by you.

Morning Reflection:

Silence can be heavy. What am I holding in that wants a voice?

Prompt:

- **What have I wanted to say lately, but haven't?**

_____
_____
_____
_____
_____
_____
_____
_____

- **Why?**

_____
_____
_____
_____
_____
_____
_____

Mindful Minute:

Breathe slowly. Imagine speaking aloud what you've buried — in a safe space, without fear.

Mantra:

"My silence deserves translation."

Evening Reflection:

- Did I hold something back today that I needed to release?

_____
_____
_____
_____
_____
_____
_____

- **How can I express it differently tomorrow?**

_____
_____
_____
_____
_____
_____
_____

Day 30: The Weight of Responsibility

You were taught that being a man meant holding it all—
the fear, the pressure, the needs of others—
without ever letting your knees buckle.

You became the steady one.
The reliable one.
The one who doesn't flinch, doesn't falter,
doesn't ask for help.

But responsibility without rest becomes a quiet cage.
You weren't meant to carry everything alone.
Strength isn't in how much you hold—
it's in knowing when to set it down.

Morning Reflection:

Responsibility doesn't have to mean carrying it all alone.

Prompt:

- **Where have I taken on more than I can manage?**

_____
_____
_____
_____
_____
_____
_____

Mindful Minute:

With each breath, imagine placing one responsibility outside yourself — not gone, but no longer pressing.

Mantra:

"It's okay to share the weight."

Evening Reflection:

- **Did I feel overwhelmed today?**

_____
_____
_____
_____
_____
_____
_____

Day 31: The Unseen Grief

Some losses don't come with funerals.
They come with silence, detachment, or pretending not to care.
They live in the pauses between "I'm fine" and what you really meant.

Maybe it was a father who was physically there but emotionally absent.
A childhood joy that no one noticed fading.
Dreams you buried to survive.

Grief isn't always loud.
Sometimes, it lingers in the corners of your life,
waiting for permission to be felt.

You don't have to justify your sadness.
Your heart remembers what your mind tried to forget.
Give that grief a name—
and the space to breathe.

Morning Reflection:

Grief doesn't always wear black. Sometimes it hides in numbness, restlessness, or anger.

Prompt:

- **What have I lost — recently or long ago — that I haven't fully grieved?**

_____
_____
_____
_____
_____
_____
_____
_____
_____
_____
_____
_____
_____
_____
_____
_____

Mindful Minute:

Hold your heart gently in thought. Let a wave of unspoken grief rise and pass, like breath.

Mantra:

"My grief is real, even if unspoken."

Evening Reflection:

- **Did I notice grief's presence today — even in subtle forms?**

_____
_____
_____
_____
_____
_____
_____

Day 32: Unlabeled Emotions

Not everything you feel has a name—
and that's okay.

There are days you wake up heavy without a story,
restless without a reason,
tender without a trigger.

Men are often taught to make sense of everything—
to explain, fix, or ignore what they can't define.
But not every emotion shows up with clarity.

Sometimes, your body speaks in sensations:
tight chest, clenched jaw, tired soul.
Sometimes, your heart speaks in silence.

You don't need to label it to feel it.
You just need to slow down long enough to listen.
Let the unnamed parts of you be known.

Morning Reflection:

Some feelings don't have names, only tension. Today, let's listen to what they're trying to say.

Prompt:

- **Where in my body do I feel something unclear?**

_____
_____
_____
_____
_____
_____
_____
_____

Mindful Minute:

Do a full body scan. Pause at any tightness. Greet it with curiosity instead of judgment.

Mantra:

"Even unnamed feelings deserve compassion."

Evening Reflection:

- **Did I feel anything today that I couldn't explain? How did I respond?**

_____
_____
_____
_____
_____
_____
_____

Day 33: The Invisible Mental Load

You remember the birthdays.
You anticipate the problems.
You carry the unspoken responsibilities no one notices—
until you drop one.

The mental load is more than stress;
it's the constant, invisible labor of managing everything
and everyone.
And men carry it, too—silently, often without
acknowledgment.

Because being "strong" meant handling it.
Being dependable meant not complaining.
Being a man meant holding it all.

But even mental strength has a capacity.
You were never meant to hold it all alone.

Release isn't weakness.
Asking for help isn't a failure.
Naming the weight you carry is the first step to finally
breathing again.

Morning Reflection:

Mental clutter can wear us down. Today, honor your mind's labor.

Prompt:

- **What thoughts or tasks have been circling in my mind this week?**

_____
_____
_____
_____
_____
_____
_____
_____

- **Can I write them down — or let some go?**

_____
_____
_____
_____
_____
_____
_____
_____
_____

Mindful Minute:

Visualize your thoughts as floating leaves. Let each one drift by without grabbing it.

Mantra:

"My mind deserves rest."

Evening Reflection:

- Was I mentally overloaded today?

_____
_____
_____
_____
_____
_____
_____
_____

- What can I simplify moving forward?

_____
_____
_____
_____
_____
_____
_____
_____

Day 34: Carrying Generational Baggage

Some of the weight you carry was never yours to begin with.

You were handed beliefs, fears, habits— passed down like heirlooms wrapped in silence.

"Men don't cry."
"Work first, feel later."
"Love is earned, not given."

You didn't choose these narratives,
but you've been living them.

Carrying what your father never unpacked.
Repeating what your grandfather never questioned.
Surviving what they couldn't speak of.

This baggage doesn't make you weak.
It makes you human.
And now—aware—you have the power to put it down.

You get to choose what continues
and what ends with you.

Morning Reflection:

You may be carrying things your father, grandfather, or lineage never got to put down.

Prompt:

- **What generational patterns or beliefs might I be carrying unconsciously?**

_____
_____
_____
_____
_____
_____
_____

Mindful Minute:

Close your eyes and imagine handing back a weight that was never yours to carry.

Mantra:

"I am allowed to break the cycle."

Evening Reflection:

- **Did I repeat or resist an old family pattern today?**

_____
_____
_____
_____
_____
_____
_____

- **How did it affect me?**

_____
_____
_____
_____
_____
_____
_____
_____

Day 35 – Giving Myself Permission

I don't need a crisis to rest.
I don't need someone else's approval to feel.
I don't need to earn softness or justify my peace.

Today, I give myself permission—
to be tired without guilt,
to feel joy without fear,
to cry without shame,
to say no without apology.

No one handed me this permission slip.
I had to write it myself.
And maybe that's the kind of power that matters most—
the quiet, liberating kind
that says: *I belong to myself now.*

Morning Reflection:

Sometimes the permission you've been waiting for… is your own.

Prompt:

- **What do I need to give myself permission for today — to feel, do, say, or stop?**

_____
_____
_____
_____
_____
_____
_____
_____

Mindful Minute:

Place a hand on your heart and whisper: "I give myself permission to be fully human."

Mantra:

"I give myself what I've been waiting for."

Evening Reflection:

- **Did I withhold permission from myself today? What might shift if I allowed it?**

_____
_____
_____
_____
_____
_____
_____

WEEK 6: GRIEF YOU NEVER CLAIMED

This week is for the grief that went unspoken — the small and large losses you were told to "man up" through. You don't need to justify your pain to feel it. Grief isn't weakness; it's a sign that something mattered.

Day 36: The Grief I Didn't Acknowledge

There were losses I never named.
Disappointments I shrugged off.
Parts of me that vanished quietly—
and I kept going like nothing happened.

I told myself, "It wasn't that deep."
But it was.
I carried endings without closure,
silences that felt like abandonment,
shifts that left me disoriented.

Grief doesn't always come with tears or funerals.
Sometimes it shows up as numbness, anger, or withdrawal.
Today, I name what I've lost—
and I give myself permission to feel it.

Acknowledging it doesn't make me weak.
It makes me human.
And maybe, for the first time,
it makes me whole.

Morning Reflection:

Not all grief is loud. Some grief live in quiet corners.

Prompt:

- **What loss have I quietly endured without giving myself time to feel it?**

_____
_____
_____
_____
_____
_____
_____
_____

Mindful Minute:

Place both hands over your chest. Breathe into the space beneath them, holding yourself gently.

Mantra:

"My silent grief still matters."

Evening Reflection:

- **Did I notice a grief that surfaced today — even briefly?**

_____
_____
_____
_____
_____
_____
_____
_____

Day 37: Mourning Who I Was Supposed to Be

There's a version of me that never existed—
the man I thought I had to become.
Always composed. Always capable. Always in control.
I built him in my mind, brick by brick,
using other people's expectations as mortar.

I chased that version for years.
And every time I didn't measure up,
I called it failure.
But maybe it was just misdirection.

Today, I mourn who I was *supposed* to be—
not out of regret,
but to free myself from the weight of unrealistic ideals.

The man I am is not a consolation prize.
He's a reclamation.
One choice, one breath, one truth at a time.

Morning Reflection:

Grief can come from letting go of the version of yourself you were once chasing.

Prompt:

- **What part of the man I thought I'd become do I need to grieve and release?**

_____
_____
_____
_____
_____
_____
_____
_____

Mindful Minute:

Breathe in acceptance. Breathe out expectation. Repeat.

Mantra:

"I honor who I was, and who I'm becoming."

Evening Reflection:

- Did I feel at peace with my past today — or did it weigh on me?

_____
_____
_____
_____
_____
_____
_____

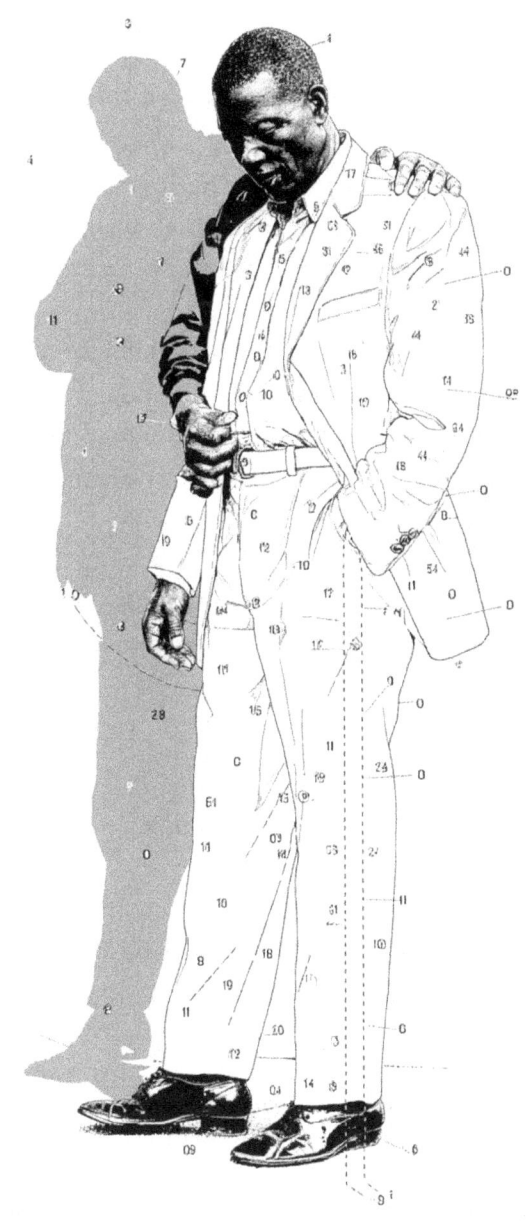

Day 38: Unprocessed Loss

There are losses we never gave ourselves permission to grieve—moments, people, opportunities, even versions of ourselves we silently buried. Not every wound bled in public, and not every goodbye was spoken aloud. But still, the ache remained.

Unprocessed loss lingers in the body like a forgotten song—familiar, heavy, and unfinished. As men, we often move forward without pause, carrying sorrow in hidden ways. But healing asks us to stop. To look back. To name what we lost and allow it to matter.

You don't have to stay stoic. You're allowed to mourn the things that didn't get closure. You're allowed to feel. Even now.

Morning Reflection:

We move on so quickly. But the body remembers what we rushed past.

Prompt:

- **Is there a loss I never slowed down to feel?**

_____
_____
_____
_____
_____
_____
_____

- **What would it mean to revisit it — with care?**

_____
_____
_____
_____
_____
_____
_____

Mindful Minute:

Imagine sitting beside your younger self in a moment of loss. Be with him, not to fix, but to witness.

Mantra:

"I am safe enough to feel."

Evening Reflection:

- **Did I allow any old feelings to surface today? How did I respond?**

_____
_____
_____
_____
_____
_____
_____

Day 39: Grieving Alone

So many of us learned to grieve in silence—to retreat into ourselves when pain became too heavy to share. We swallowed our sorrow and wore strength like armor, convincing the world we were fine. But grief held alone becomes something else. It becomes isolation.

To grieve alone is not just about the absence of others—it's about the absence of permission. The kind that says, *You're allowed to break here. You're allowed to not have the words yet.*

You don't have to carry your losses in solitude. Your grief is valid. Your tears don't make you weak. You are not less of a man for needing someone to sit with you in the dark.

Morning Reflection:

You don't have to grieve in silence. You never did.

Prompt:

- Where have I grieved in isolation?

_____
_____
_____
_____
_____
_____
_____

- Who might I trust to hold space with me?

_____
_____
_____
_____
_____
_____
_____

Mindful Minute:

Picture someone safe sitting with you — saying nothing, just present. Let that be enough.

Mantra:

"I don't have to grieve alone."

Evening Reflection:

- **Did I reach out today — or wish I had?**

_____
_____
_____
_____
_____
_____
_____

- **What kept me from doing so?**

_____
_____
_____
_____
_____
_____
_____

Day 40: Micro-Griefs

Not all grief arrives like thunder. Some come quietly—small losses we don't know how to name. The friend who stopped calling. The job we stayed in too long. The childhood joy we can't seem to access anymore. These are micro-griefs—tiny fractures in our daily living that accumulate over time.

They often go unacknowledged because they don't seem *big enough* to mourn. But they matter. They shape how we show up. They influence what we believe we deserve.

Today, give space to the subtle losses. Let them rise. Let them speak. Healing doesn't only come from mourning the monumental—it begins when we honor even the quietest goodbyes.

Morning Reflection:

Sometimes we grieve the moments — not just the milestones.

Prompt:

- **What little griefs have I been brushing off— friendships faded, missed chances, old dreams?**

_____
_____
_____
_____
_____
_____
_____
_____

Mindful Minute:

Say to yourself: "Even the small things mattered." Let that truth land softly.

Mantra:

"Even the little losses deserve my care."

Evening Reflection:

- **Did I honor any "small" griefs today?**

_____
_____
_____
_____
_____
_____
_____

- **What did that feel like?**

  _____
  _____
  _____
  _____
  _____
  _____
  _____
  _____

Day 41: Making Space for Mourning

We often rush through loss—not because we don't feel it, but because we don't know where to place it. Mourning has no convenient schedule, and grief doesn't follow a clean arc. In a world that demands we "move on," creating space to mourn feels rebellious.

But mourning is not weakness. It's an act of remembrance. A way to honor what mattered. Whether it's the loss of a loved one, a missed opportunity, or a version of yourself you had to let go of, grief deserves room to unfold.

Today, give yourself permission to pause. To breathe. To remember. Mourning is a sacred space where healing begins.

Morning Reflection:

Healing begins when we stop rushing our mourning process.

Prompt:

- **What ritual or gesture can I create this week to honor something I lost?**

_____
_____
_____
_____
_____
_____
_____

Mindful Minute:

Light an imaginary candle in your mind. Sit beside it. Let it symbolize your right to mourn.

Mantra:

"I give myself sacred space to mourn."

Evening Reflection:

- **Did I give grief time and space today — or avoid it?**

_____
_____
_____
_____
_____
_____
_____
_____

Day 42: Honoring My Emotional Survival

There are parts of you that kept going when it didn't make sense to. Strategies that once protected you. Silence that shielded you. Anger that gave you power when you felt powerless. Disconnection that kept the pain manageable.

Maybe they don't serve you now—but they did, once. And that deserves respect.

Emotional survival isn't always graceful, but it is always brave. You made it here because something inside you chose to endure. Before you ask yourself to change, thank yourself for surviving. That, too, is healing.

Morning Reflection:

Every unshed tear, every swallowed pain — you survived it. That matters.

Prompt:

- How did I survive emotionally in hard seasons?

_____
_____
_____
_____
_____
_____
_____

- Can I name that strength and honor it?

_____
_____
_____
_____
_____
_____
_____
_____

Mindful Minute:

Place a hand on your heart and whisper: "Thank you for surviving."

Mantra:

"I survived. That means something."

Evening Reflection:

- **Did I reflect on how far I've come today?**

  _____
  _____
  _____
  _____
  _____
  _____
  _____
  _____

- **What am I proud of, quietly?**

  _____
  _____
  _____
  _____
  _____
  _____
  _____
  _____

WEEK 7: THE PROTECTOR REDEFINED

This week invites you to re-imagine what it means to protect — not from a place of hyper-vigilance or detachment, but from grounded strength. The truest protection is presence, not control. It starts with you, and it extends with love.

Day 43: Redefining Strength

Strength isn't just holding it all together. It's not just grinding through the hard days, or showing no emotion when everything inside you aches.

Real strength is the courage to be honest. To feel. To ask for help. To rest without guilt. To face the truth of your story without shame.

It's choosing growth over appearance. Wholeness over performance. Vulnerability over silence.

This kind of strength doesn't shout—it steadies. It doesn't pretend—it reveals. And it doesn't isolate—it connects.

You've always been strong. Now, you're just defining it on your own terms.

Morning Reflection:

- What if strength isn't how hard I hit, but how open I can stay?

_____
_____
_____
_____
_____
_____
_____

Prompt:

- In what ways have I confused protection with emotional shutdown?

_____
_____
_____
_____
_____
_____
_____

Mindful Minute:

Inhale slowly, saying inwardly "I am strong." Exhale slowly, saying "I am soft." Repeat 3x.

Mantra:

"My softness is strength."

Evening Reflection:

- **Was there a moment today I let my guard down and stayed present?**

_____
_____
_____
_____
_____
_____
_____
_____

Day 44: Who Am I Protecting?

Sometimes, the armor we wear was never for battle—but for hiding. We protect others from our truth, protect ourselves from rejection, protect our image from cracking.

But in all that protecting, we can lose sight of what we're really guarding: our pain, our tenderness, our unmet needs.

Ask yourself today—who am I protecting? And is it costing me connection, healing, or freedom?

Protection without reflection becomes isolation. You deserve to be safe, yes—but also known. Let someone see what's underneath.

Morning Reflection:

We often protect others — but neglect to protect ourselves.

Prompt:

- Who or what have I spent my life protecting?

_____
_____
_____
_____
_____
_____
_____
_____

Mindful Minute:

Wrap your arms around yourself and breathe deeply. Imagine giving safety to your inner child.

Mantra:

"I protect myself with love, not walls."

Evening Reflection:

Did I choose myself today — in thought, boundary, or action?

Day 45: The Fear Beneath Protection

Protection often masks fear—the fear of not being enough, of being judged, of being abandoned if you're fully seen. So we hide behind toughness, humor, busyness, or silence.

But the real strength isn't in the armor. It's in confronting the fear underneath it.

Today, notice where your protection is fear in disguise. And gently remind yourself: being vulnerable doesn't make you weak—it makes you real. And real is where healing begins.

Morning Reflection:

Every overreaction has a root fear it's covering.

Prompt:

- **When I get controlling, what fear is usually behind it?**

_____
_____
_____
_____
_____
_____
_____
_____

Mindful Minute:

Notice your body's tension — jaw, shoulders, fists. Gently release one at a time with each breath.

Mantra:

"I see the fear and respond with compassion."

Evening Reflection:

- **What fear surfaced today? How did I respond?**

_____
_____
_____
_____
_____
_____
_____
_____

Day 46: The Protector Within

There's a part of you that has always tried to keep you safe — by staying quiet, staying small, or staying strong for everyone else.

This inner protector isn't your enemy. It's a younger version of you doing the best they could with what they had. But now, you're older. Wiser. And you get to choose new ways of protecting yourself that don't require self-abandonment.

Today, thank that inner protector. Then ask: what does protection look like when it's rooted in love, not fear?

Morning Reflection:

There's a wise part of me that doesn't need to prove anything. He simply protects by being.

Prompt:

- **What does the grounded, emotionally safe protector version of me look and feel like?**

_____
_____
_____
_____
_____
_____
_____
_____

Mindful Minute:

Close your eyes. Imagine that protector version of yourself standing beside you. Let him guide your breath.

Mantra:

"I protect with presence, not pressure."

Evening Reflection:

- Did I show up today in a way my inner protector would be proud of?

_____
_____
_____
_____
_____
_____
_____

Day 47: Boundaries Are Protection, Too

You don't need to be harsh to protect yourself. Boundaries are not walls — they're doors with locks, knobs, and the choice to open or close them.

Setting limits isn't selfish; it's a sacred act of self-respect. It tells others how to love you and reminds you that your peace matters.

Today, consider where you've been overexposed, overreaching, or overgiving. Protection doesn't always roar. Sometimes, it simply says, "That's enough."

Morning Reflection:

Setting boundaries isn't pushing people away. It's inviting them to meet you in respect.

Prompt:

- **Where in my life do I need to establish or reinforce boundaries?**

_____
_____
_____
_____
_____
_____
_____
_____

Mindful Minute:

Breathe deeply and say: "I am worthy of space." Let the words echo internally.

Mantra:

"My boundaries are an act of love."

Evening Reflection:

Was there a boundary I honored today — or wished I had?

Day 48: Safety over Secrecy

We were taught to keep things in. To lock away the truth, the tears, the trembling. But secrecy is a heavy armor — and it keeps out what could heal us, too.

There is strength in being seen. In finding spaces where your truth is safe, not silenced. Where your story can stretch out and breathe.

Today, ask yourself: am I protecting myself, or hiding myself? Safety allows freedom. Secrecy, over time, becomes a cage.

Morning Reflection:

You don't have to keep secrets to feel safe. Vulnerability can be a new form of protection.

Prompt:

- What have I been hiding in the name of strength — and what would safety look like instead?

_____
_____
_____
_____
_____
_____
_____
_____

Mindful Minute:

Inhale: "I am safe now." Exhale: "I can be seen." Repeat until the tension lowers.

Mantra:

"Being seen is not unsafe."

Evening Reflection:

- **Did I feel safe enough to be honest today — with myself or someone else?**

_____
_____
_____
_____
_____
_____
_____
_____

Day 49: Protecting My Peace

Peace isn't passive. It's not just the absence of noise — it's the presence of clarity, boundaries, and self-honoring choices.

You don't have to explain why you guard your rest, your joy, your inner quiet. Every time you choose peace over proving, stillness over struggle, you're rebuilding yourself.

Today, protect your peace like it's sacred. Because it is.

Morning Reflection:

Not everything deserves your reaction. Sometimes, silence is self-defense.

Prompt:

- What robs me of peace — and what would it look like to reclaim it?

_____
_____
_____
_____
_____
_____
_____
_____

Mindful Minute:

Picture yourself standing in a quiet field. No noise, no pressure.

Just breath and space.

Mantra:

"My peace is non-negotiable."

Evening Reflection:

- **Did I defend my peace today?**

_____
_____
_____
_____
_____
_____
_____
_____

WEEK 8: THE INNER BOY STILL NEEDS YOU

The boy you were still lives within. He's not weak. He's wounded. This week is about reconnecting with your inner child — not to pity him, but to listen, to hold, and to begin healing where the first cracks formed.

Day 50: Meet the Boy Again

Before the performance, the silence, and the armor — there was a boy. Curious. Soft. Honest. Open.

He wasn't broken. He was shaped. Taught to survive before he could simply be.

Today, meet him again. Not to fix him, but to listen. To remind him that he still belongs. That he's still here — under all the layers, waiting to be welcomed back home.

Morning Reflection:

Before I became a man, I was a boy with needs, dreams, and wounds.

Prompt:

- **If I could meet the 8-year-old version of myself, what would I want him to know?**

_____
_____
_____
_____
_____
_____
_____
_____

Mindful Minute:

Close your eyes. Picture him sitting across from you.

Breathe slowly and say: **"You are safe. I'm here now."**

Mantra:

"I remember you. I see you."

Evening Reflection:

- **Did I treat myself with the gentleness my younger self needed?**

_____
_____
_____
_____
_____
_____
_____
_____

Day 51: He Didn't Deserve That

There are moments in your story that you've minimized, excused, or buried. But the truth remains: he didn't deserve that.

The boy you once were — the one who was silenced, shamed, overlooked — needed safety, not strength. He needed presence, not performance.

Today, let that truth settle in. Honor his pain without justifying it. Hold space for his wounds without rushing to explain them away.

Because healing starts when we stop rewriting what hurt us — and begin believing that we never deserved the hurt.

Morning Reflection:

What happened to me wasn't always fair, and that's not my fault.

Prompt:

- **What memory still carries shame or confusion?**

_____
_____
_____
_____
_____
_____
_____
_____

Mindful Minute:

Place a hand over your heart. Inhale forgiveness. Exhale blame. Repeat gently.

Mantra:

"It wasn't my fault. And I'm healing."

Evening Reflection:

- **What old story or shame showed up today? How did I respond?**

_____
_____
_____
_____
_____
_____
_____

Day 52: What Did He Need?

Before the tough skin and the quiet pretending, there was a boy with real needs — for comfort, for being seen, for softness without shame.

Not strength. Not stoicism. Not perfection.

He needed to be held when he cried. To be told he was good even when he failed. To be asked, not ordered.

Today, ask yourself gently: *What did he need that he never got?*

And then, as the man you are now — begin to give him just that.

Morning Reflection:

Emotional neglect doesn't always look like abuse — but it still leaves wounds.

Prompt:

- **What did my younger self need more of — love, affirmation, safety, permission?**

_____
_____
_____
_____
_____
_____
_____
_____

Mindful Minute:

Whisper softly: "You deserved more."

Let your breath hold that truth.

Mantra:

"I give myself what I never received."

Evening Reflection:

- **How did I show up for my needs today, without apology?**

_____
_____
_____
_____
_____
_____
_____

Day 53: No One Was There

There were moments when the world went silent around your pain. When your voice trembled but no one heard. When you needed someone — and no one showed up.

That absence left a mark. A loneliness that didn't always feel loud, but always felt *real*.

It's okay to name it now. To say, *"No one was there, and it hurt."*

You're not weak for admitting that. You're healing. Because being honest about the loneliness is the first step in no longer carrying it alone.

Morning Reflection:

There are parts of my past no one witnessed. That doesn't mean they weren't real.

Prompt:

- **Where in my life did I feel invisible — and what did I wish someone had said or done?**

_____
_____
_____
_____
_____
_____
_____
_____

Mindful Minute:

Picture a younger version of you being held, comforted, and believed.

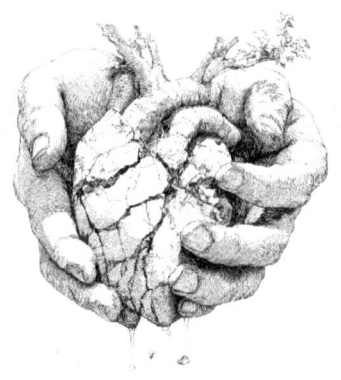

Mantra:

"My pain was real. And it matters."

Evening Reflection:

- **Did I validate an emotion today I once suppressed?**

_____
_____
_____
_____
_____
_____
_____
_____

Day 54: He Needed Play

Before the weight of expectations, before the silence became armor — he needed play.
He needed space to be messy, loud, curious, and joyful.

But maybe that boy had to grow up too fast. Maybe he was praised more for being responsible than for being *alive*.

Reclaim that now. Give yourself permission to laugh, to rest, to explore without purpose.
Play is not a luxury — it's a return. A return to the parts of you that never stopped wanting to be free.

Morning Reflection:

Masculinity doesn't have to be serious all the time. Play is healing, too.

Prompt:

- **When was the last time I felt playful, spontaneous, or creative? What's stopping me now?**

_____
_____
_____
_____
_____
_____
_____
_____

Mindful Minute:

Smile for no reason. Let it sit on your face, even if it feels odd. That's part of the healing.

Mantra:

"I give myself permission to play."

Evening Reflection:

- **What moment today felt light or joyful? Did I let myself enjoy it?**

_____
_____
_____
_____
_____
_____
_____

Day 55: Not Weak for Wanting Comfort

Wanting to be held, understood, or simply not feel alone — that doesn't make you weak.
It makes you human.

Somewhere along the line, many of us were taught that comfort was a crutch. That needing softness made us less of a man.
But strength doesn't mean self-denial.

You are not less for craving warmth, touch, or reassurance. You are more — because you are finally allowing yourself to need, and to be met in that need.

Morning Reflection:

Crying wasn't weakness. Wanting affection wasn't weakness. It was human.

Prompt:

- **What comforting gestures did I long for as a boy — and where can I create that now?**

_____
_____
_____
_____
_____
_____
_____
_____

Mindful Minute:

Hug yourself. Really. Wrap your arms around your shoulders and breathe in calm.

Mantra:

"I am worthy of comfort."

Evening Reflection:

- **Did I give or receive comfort today — or deny myself the chance?**

_____
_____
_____
_____
_____
_____
_____
_____

Day 56: I Am the Father Now

There comes a quiet moment when you realize — the father you waited for, wished for, imagined... is you.
You are the one who now carries the responsibility, not just for others, but for yourself.

To guide. To protect. To affirm. To forgive.
Not perfectly, but presently.

This is your chance to reparent the parts of you still longing.
To become the man you needed — and offer him to yourself first.

Morning Reflection:

The boy within still waits for a protector. I get to be that man now.

Prompt:

How can I show up today as the father figure I wish I had?

_____
_____
_____
_____
_____
_____
_____
_____

Mindful Minute:

Stand tall. Breathe into your spine.

Say inwardly: "I've got you. Always."

Mantra:

"I am the protector I once needed."

Evening Reflection:

- How did I father myself today? Where can I do even better tomorrow?

Month 2 Reflection: Inner Shifts

1. **What I Released / What I Claimed**

- What beliefs, habits, or fears did you release?

_____
_____
_____
_____
_____
_____
_____
_____

WEEK 9: EMOTIONAL LANGUAGE FOR MEN

Men are often taught to feel only in extremes: **anger or silence**. But there is a full emotional vocabulary waiting for us — words that build bridges to understanding, healing, and connection. This week, we begin to name our emotions. When you can name it, you can face it.

Day 57: More than Angry

Anger is often the loudest emotion we allow ourselves to feel —
but beneath it, there is usually something softer: hurt, fear, disappointment, grief.

You're not just angry.
You're carrying pain that was never named.

Today, instead of pushing it away, get curious.
What's beneath the anger?
What are you really trying to say?

You're allowed to feel it all — not just what looks powerful on the outside.

Morning Reflection:

Anger is often the bodyguard of unspoken emotions.

Prompt:

- **When was the last time I felt angry?**

_____
_____
_____
_____
_____
_____
_____

- **What was beneath it — hurt, fear, shame, rejection?**

_____
_____
_____
_____
_____
_____
_____
_____

Mindful Minute:

Breathe slowly and ask yourself: What am I really feeling right now?

Mantra:

"There is more beneath my anger."

Evening Reflection:

- **Did I pause to name what I felt before reacting?**

_____
_____
_____
_____
_____
_____
_____

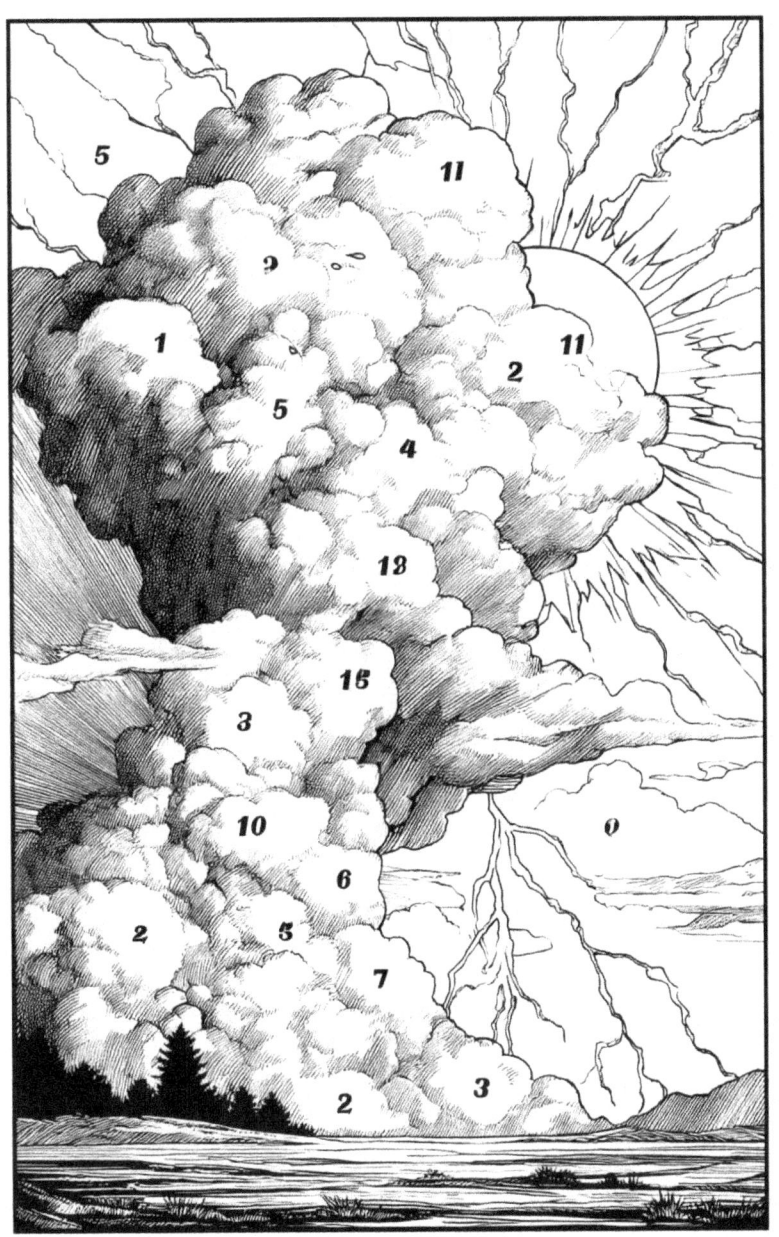

Day 58: Expand the Vocabulary

Many of us grew up with only a few emotional words:
angry, fine, tired.
But your heart speaks in a richer language — it knows
disappointment, shame, peace, longing, relief, pride, joy.

The more words you have, the more permission you give yourself to feel,
to understand, and to communicate clearly.

Today, pause and ask:
What am I really feeling?
Not just the surface, but the layer underneath.

You don't need to master it overnight.
Just start naming your truth — one word at a time.

Morning Reflection:

Having words for your feelings doesn't make you weak —
it makes you wise.

Prompt:

- **How many feeling words can I name without judgment? (e.g., disappointed, anxious, lonely, proud, tender)**

_____
_____
_____
_____
_____
_____
_____

Mindful Minute:

Scan your body. Name three emotions present — even if they feel small or messy.

Mantra:

"My emotions have names. I honor them."

Evening Reflection:

- Did I notice any emotional shifts today? How did I respond to them?

_____
_____
_____
_____
_____
_____
_____

Day 59: It's Okay to Not Know

There's pressure — spoken and unspoken — for men to always have the answers.
To know what's next. To lead with certainty. To never stumble or pause.

But real growth often begins in the space of **not knowing**.
In the humility of saying, *"I don't have it all figured out."*

You're not less of a man because you're still learning.
You're human because you're open.

Let yourself sit with the questions today.
Let curiosity lead instead of certainty.
You're allowed to be unsure — and still worthy.

Morning Reflection:

If I wasn't taught how to name my feelings, I can learn now.

Prompt:

- **Which emotions confuse or overwhelm me?**

_____
_____
_____
_____
_____
_____
_____

- **Which ones was I taught to suppress?**

_____
_____
_____
_____
_____
_____
_____

Mindful Minute:

Close your eyes and gently say:

"Whatever I feel is valid, even when it doesn't make sense yet."

Mantra:

"I can feel without fully understanding."

Evening Reflection:

- **What emotion today surprised me?**

_____
_____
_____
_____
_____
_____
_____

- **What did I do with it?**

_____
_____
_____
_____
_____
_____
_____

Day 60: Emotional Safety Begins With Me

Emotional safety isn't just about the spaces we walk into — it's also about the space we create within ourselves.

Too often, men learn to suppress rather than soothe, to harden rather than hold. But healing asks something different: that we become a safe place for our own emotions to land.

That we learn to respond to pain with compassion, not punishment.
To meet discomfort with patience, not shame.
To say to ourselves, *"You're allowed to feel this. You're safe here."*

Emotional safety begins when you stop abandoning yourself.
When you become the home you never had.

Morning Reflection:

When I judge my feelings, I abandon myself.

Prompt:

- Where in my life do I feel emotionally unsafe — and what boundaries or support could change that?

_____
_____
_____
_____
_____
_____
_____

Mindful Minute:

Place your hand over your chest. Say silently, "You're allowed to feel."

Mantra:

"I create safety for my emotions."

Evening Reflection:

- **Was I emotionally honest with myself today?**

_____
_____
_____
_____
_____
_____
_____

- **With others?**

_____
_____
_____
_____
_____
_____
_____
_____

Day 61: Naming the Feeling, Not the Story

When pain rises, we often rush to make sense of it — spinning stories, assigning blame, searching for a neat conclusion. But healing doesn't always begin with logic. Sometimes, it begins with presence.

Instead of asking, *"Why do I feel this way?"*
Try asking, *"What is this feeling?"*

Naming the feeling — anger, sadness, fear, shame, joy — without attaching it to a narrative helps you sit with the emotion rather than escape it.
It reminds you that emotions don't have to be justified to be felt.

You don't have to solve the story to honor the truth of the feeling.

Morning Reflection:

I don't always need to explain why I feel something — I just need to notice it.

Prompt:

- **What emotion did I feel this week that I tried to rationalize away?**

_____
_____
_____
_____
_____
_____
_____
_____

Mindful Minute:

Silently name your feeling without attaching a story.

Just: "This is sadness." Breathe.

Mantra:

"Feelings first. Story second."

Evening Reflection:

- **Did I give myself permission to feel without fixing?**

_____
_____
_____
_____
_____
_____
_____

Day 62: I Don't Have to Be Stoic

There's a difference between being grounded and being hardened.
Many of us were taught that stoicism was the highest form of strength — to not flinch, to not cry, to not speak.

But stoicism, when worn like armor, becomes silence.
It hides not just your hurt, but your humanity.

You are allowed to feel.
You are allowed to tremble.
You are allowed to be seen carrying the weight, not just bearing it in silence.

Being expressive doesn't make you less of a man.
It makes you more of a whole human.

Morning Reflection:

Emotional control isn't the same as emotional repression.

Prompt:

- **What feelings do I habitually suppress in the name of control?**

_____
_____
_____
_____
_____
_____
_____

Mindful Minute:

Let your face go soft. Relax your jaw.

Say inwardly:

"I don't have to hold it all together."

Mantra:

"It's safe to be soft."

Evening Reflection:

- **Where did I let my guard down today, even slightly?**

Day 63: Words That Heal

Words can wound — but they can also mend.
The words you speak to yourself matter. The ones you withheld as a boy, and the ones you longed to hear, still echo in your chest.

Today, begin choosing language that doesn't just describe your pain but invites healing.

Say, *"I deserved better."*
Say, *"I am safe now."*
Say, *"I am learning to love without shame."*

Every healing journey needs a new vocabulary — words that meet you with softness, words that affirm your worth, and words that remind you: healing is possible.
And you are worthy of it.

Morning Reflection:

When I express my truth, I give others permission to do the same.

Prompt:

- **What is one feeling I need to express to someone (or myself) — even if I never say it out loud?**

_____
_____
_____
_____
_____
_____
_____

Mindful Minute:

Write the word of that emotion in the air with your finger.

Let it live. Let it breathe.

Mantra:

"I speak healing into my experience."

Evening Reflection:

- **What emotion needs more of my attention tomorrow?**

_____
_____
_____
_____
_____
_____
_____
_____

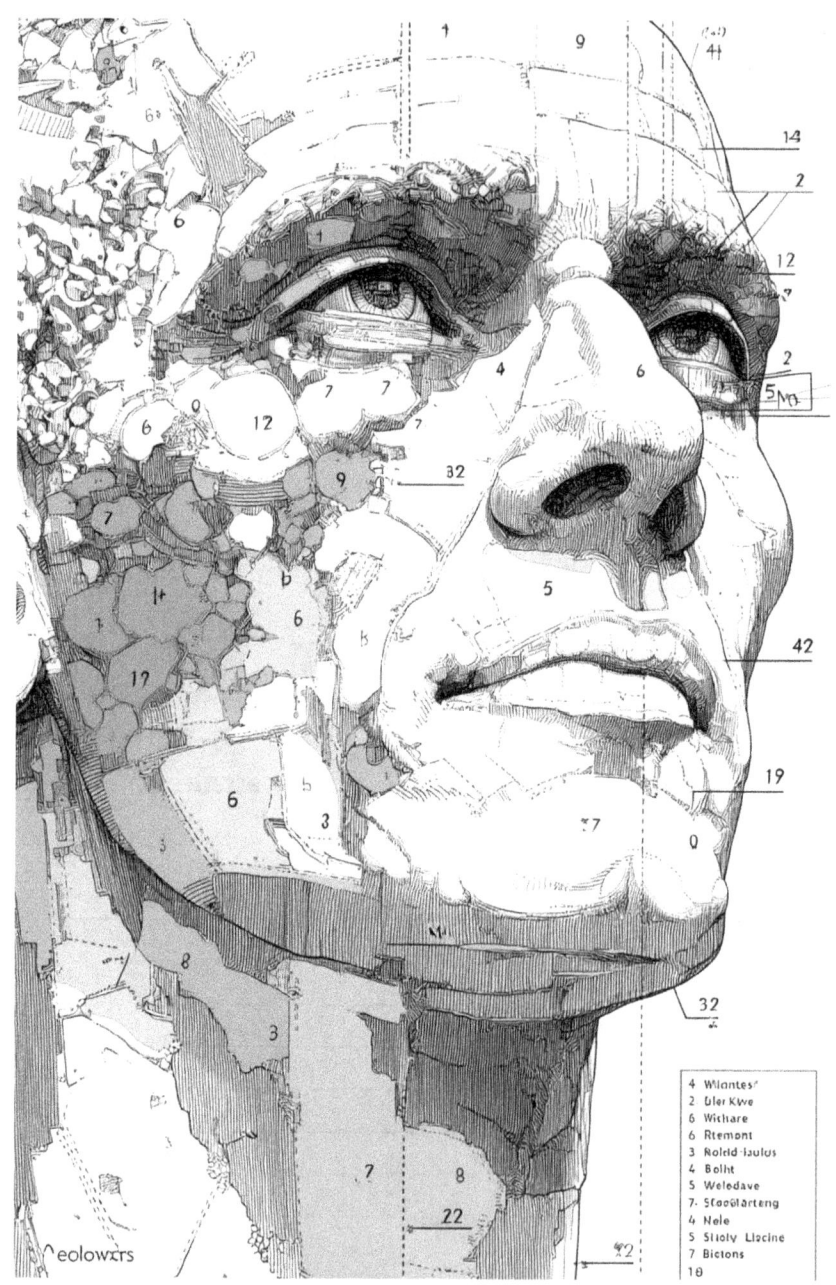

WEEK 10: SOMATIC CHECK-INS

Your body holds the truth even when your words fail. Many men live in their heads — logical, disconnected — while the body stores tension, stress, trauma, and even unspoken joy. This week is an invitation to listen to your body's signals. Your healing is not just in the mind. It's also in the body.

Day 64: My Body Speaks

Before you had words, you had sensations.
Long before you could articulate grief or joy, your body carried it.
Tight shoulders, clenched jaws, shallow breaths — your body has been whispering truths you didn't feel safe enough to say aloud.

Today, pay attention.
That fatigue, that tension, that ache — it's not random. It's communication.

Your body is not betraying you; it's trying to reach you.
To help you notice.
To bring you back.

What is it saying?
Where is it asking you to slow down, to release, to soften?

Listen.
You deserve to feel safe *in* yourself — not just around others.

Morning Reflection:

My body often feels what my mind avoids.

Prompt:

- **Where do I carry stress, sadness, or fear in my body?**

_____
_____
_____
_____
_____
_____
_____

Mindful Minute:

Gently scan from head to toe. Linger on areas of tightness or warmth. Just observe.

Mantra:

"My body tells the truth."

Evening Reflection:

Did my body speak to me today? Did I listen?

Day 65: Shoulders Down, Heart Open

You've held so much for so long.

The world taught you to brace — to carry, to endure, to press forward even when your spirit asked you to pause. But today, you get to do it differently.

Drop your shoulders.
Not because there's nothing to carry,
but because you're allowed to carry it differently.

You don't have to harden to be strong.
You don't have to close off to be safe.

Let your heart stay open — even if it quivers.
Softness doesn't make you weak;
it means you're still human.
Still here. Still choosing presence.

Today, let your breath lower your guard.
Let peace enter the places tension once ruled.

Morning Reflection:

I hold the world on my shoulders — and it shows.

Prompt:

- **What burden am I physically carrying today? Can I release some of it?**

_____
_____
_____
_____
_____
_____
_____

Mindful Minute:

Roll your shoulders back, breathe in deeply, and exhale with sound. Notice the shift.

Mantra:

"I am not a burden bearer alone."

Evening Reflection:

- **Did I allow myself to feel supported — physically or emotionally?**

_____
_____
_____
_____
_____
_____
_____

Day 66: The Gut Feeling

There's a knowing within you —
quiet, steady, and often overlooked.

Call it instinct, intuition, your gut…
It has always been there,
whispering truths before your mind could catch up.

But years of second-guessing, of being told to "man up,"
have trained you to silence it.
To reason over feeling.
To ignore what your body already knows.

Today is an invitation to listen again.

Not everything needs to make logical sense to be real.
Your discomfort is data.
Your unease is a message.
Your gut is wise.

The more you honor that inner voice,
the more you'll realize —
you were never lost.
You just weren't listening.

Morning Reflection:

Your gut knows before your brain can explain.

Prompt:

- **What decision or situation am I facing? What does my gut say?**

_____
_____
_____
_____
_____
_____
_____

Mindful Minute:

Place a hand over your stomach. Inhale slowly. Ask silently, "What truth is here?"

Mantra:

"I trust the wisdom of my body."

Evening Reflection:

Did I honor my instincts today?

Day 67: Breath as a Messenger

Your breath carries more than air.
It carries memory, tension, fear, safety —
and signals that often go unnoticed.

A shallow breath may whisper,
"I'm bracing for something." A
held breath may murmur, "I'm
not safe here."
A deep, open breath says,
"I've returned to myself."

Breath is your first language.
Before words, before wounds,
you inhaled and exhaled —
alive, connected, whole.

You don't have to chase healing.
Sometimes, you only need to pause
and listen to what your breath is telling you.

It's not just about calming down.
It's about coming home.

Morning Reflection:

How I breathe reveals how I live.

Prompt:

- **How has my breathing felt lately — shallow, tight, open, effortless?**

_____
_____
_____
_____
_____
_____
_____

Mindful Minute:

Take five slow breaths. On each exhale, soften a little more.

Mantra:

"My breath reconnects me."

Evening Reflection:

- Did I use my breath to ground myself today?

_____
_____
_____
_____
_____
_____
_____
_____

Day 68: The Body Keeps the Score

Your body remembers what your mind forgets.
Not every bruise shows up on skin.
Not every wound bleeds.

The tension in your jaw, the
heaviness in your chest,
the ache in your shoulders —
these are stories your body has been carrying
long before you found the words.

You may not remember the moment you decided
to shrink yourself, to stay silent, to tough it out —
but your body does.

Healing isn't just about what you think.
It's about what you feel, and where you feel it.
And it starts with listening.

Notice the signals.
Pay attention to the discomfort.
Respond with compassion.

Your body isn't betraying you.
It's trying to keep you safe.

Morning Reflection:

- **What I don't process emotionally, my body stores physically.**

_____
_____
_____
_____
_____
_____
_____

Prompt:

- **Where do I feel chronic tension or discomfort?**

_____
_____
_____
_____
_____
_____
_____
_____

- **What emotion might be hiding there?**

_____
_____
_____
_____
_____
_____
_____
_____

Mindful Minute:

Sit in stillness and gently stretch your neck and shoulders. Breathe into the tight spots.

Mantra:

"I release what no longer serves me."

Evening Reflection:

- **Did I treat my body as a friend today?**

_____
_____
_____
_____
_____
_____
_____
_____

Day 69: Rest Is Revolutionary

In a world that measures worth by output,
rest becomes a quiet rebellion.

You weren't made to hustle endlessly,
to push through pain,
to wear exhaustion like a badge of honour.

Rest is not weakness.
It is a sacred return
to your body, your breath, your being.

When you choose rest,
you choose presence.
You reclaim time from a world that tries
to steal your stillness.

You say:
I am enough, even when I am not producing.
I deserve peace, not just productivity.

Let your rest be unapologetic.
Let it be radical.
Let it remind you —
you are not a machine.
You are a man learning to be whole.

Morning Reflection:

Sometimes healing begins when I stop pushing.

Prompt:

- **What would it mean for me to truly rest — without guilt?**

_____
_____
_____
_____
_____
_____
_____
_____

Mindful Minute:

Lie down, even for 60 seconds, and let gravity hold you. Feel the support.

Mantra:

"Rest is my right."

Evening Reflection:

- **Did I give myself rest, or did I chase productivity?**

Day 70: My Body Is Home

You've been taught to live in your head —
to think through pain,
to analyze feelings,
to override exhaustion.

But your body has always been speaking.
In tension.
In tightness.
In the ache you ignore.

This body —
the one you've criticized,
pushed past limits,
called "too much" or "not enough" —
is your first home.

It holds your history,
your healing,
your humanity.

Today, place a hand on your chest.
Breathe into your ribs.
Feel your feet grounded.

Say to yourself:
I live here.
I listen here.
I am safe here.

Your body is not a battlefield.
It is not a project to fix.
It is a home to return to.
Again and again.

Morning Reflection:

My body has carried me through everything — even when I didn't love it back.

Prompt:

- **What parts of my body have I judged or ignored?**

_____
_____
_____
_____
_____
_____
_____

- **How can I offer them gratitude?**

_____
_____
_____
_____
_____
_____

Mindful Minute:

Place a hand over your chest or belly and say silently,

"Thank you for carrying me."

Mantra:

"My body is not my enemy."

Evening Reflection:

- **Did I come home to myself today?**

_____
_____
_____
_____
_____
_____
_____
_____

WEEK 11: I'M ALLOWED TO BE SEEN

Many men have mastered invisibility — emotionally, spiritually, even physically. Hiding has become safety. But healing asks us to *step into the light.* To let our full selves
— broken, bold, tender, confused, healing — be witnessed without shame. This week, we start the slow process of becoming visible… to ourselves and to others.

Day 71: I'm Here

You've done so much to keep going —
but have you stopped to just *be*?

Not to fix.
Not to achieve.
Just to notice: *I'm here.*

This breath. This body. This moment.
You're not behind.
You're not late.

You're here.
And that's enough.

Morning Reflection:

I've spent so much of life shrinking, hiding, or dimming my light.

But today, I will take up space — as I am.

Prompt:

- **In what ways have I made myself smaller to be accepted?**

_____
_____
_____
_____
_____
_____
_____

Mindful Minute:

Stand in front of a mirror. Place your hand over your heart. Say, "I see you."

Mantra:

"I am allowed to take up space."

Evening Reflection:

- **Where did I allow myself to be fully present today?**

_____
_____
_____
_____
_____
_____
_____

Day 72: Hidden Behind Strength

There's a version of strength that's all armor —
always composed, always capable, always fine.

But what if that strength is just a hiding place?
A way to mask the tenderness, the exhaustion, the need?

You don't have to keep proving you're unshakable.
Sometimes, strength looks like admitting you're tired.

You are not what you protect.
You are who needs protecting, too.

Morning Reflection:

Sometimes, I hide behind competence, humor, or stoicism
— because vulnerability feels too risky.

Prompt:

- **What masks do I wear when I don't feel safe?**

_____
_____
_____
_____
_____
_____
_____

Mindful Minute:

Sit quietly. Inhale deeply.

As you exhale, imagine one mask falling away.

Mantra:

"My strength includes softness."

Evening Reflection:

- **Did I allow someone to see a real part of me today?**

_____
_____
_____
_____
_____
_____
_____

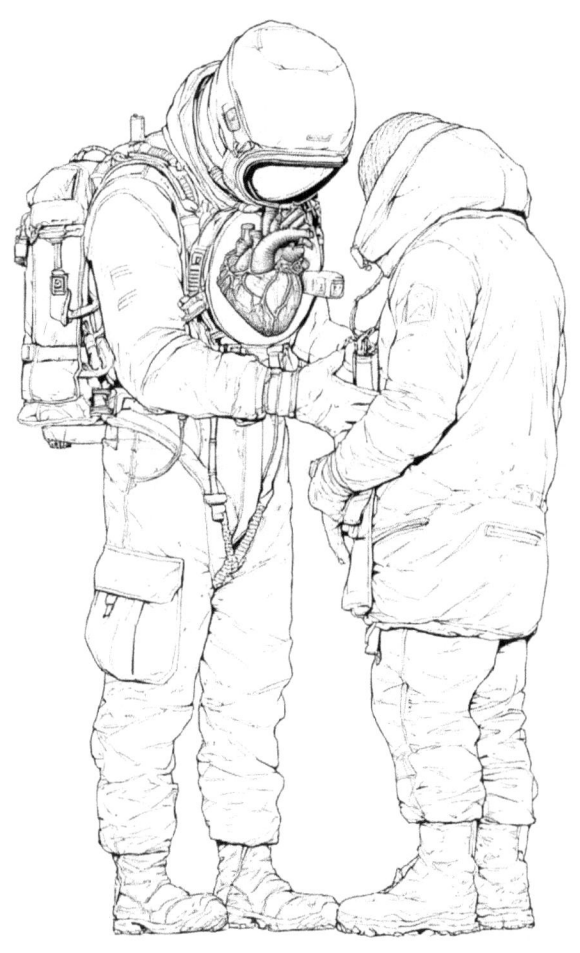

Day 73: My Inner Child Wants Witnessing

He's still there — the boy who swallowed his feelings, who tried to be brave when no one noticed the fear in his eyes.

He doesn't need fixing.
He needs to be seen, heard, and held.

Witnessing him isn't weakness — it's reconnection.
It's how you remind him: *you matter now, and you mattered then.*

Morning Reflection:

There's a boy inside me who still wonders, *"Do you see me?"*

Prompt:

- **What is one memory where I felt unseen — and what would I say to that younger me now?**

_____
_____
_____
_____
_____
_____
_____
_____

Mindful Minute:

Visualize your younger self. Sit beside him. Say: "I see you now. You're not alone."

Mantra:

"I validate the boy within."

Evening Reflection:

- **Did I show myself the care I longed for as a child?**

Day 74 – Shame Hates the Light

Shame thrives in silence and shadows.
It grows when we hide, pretend, and shrink.

But the moment you speak it — gently, honestly —
its grip loosens.

You are not your worst moment.
You are not your past.
Bring it into the light, and let healing begin.

Morning Reflection:

Shame grows in silence. But when I speak, it shrinks.

Prompt:

- **What part of me have I been too ashamed to show?**

_____
_____
_____
_____
_____
_____

- **What would it feel like to be honest about it?**

_____
_____
_____
_____
_____
_____
_____
_____

Mindful Minute:

Write one sentence you've never said out loud. Whisper it to yourself now — safely.

Mantra:

"My truth deserves air."

Evening Reflection:

- **Did I move one step closer to honesty with myself or someone else today?**

_____
_____
_____
_____
_____
_____
_____
_____

Day 75: Safe to Be Seen

You've spent years managing perception —
being what was needed, hiding what was real.

But your healing begins the moment you realize:
you deserve to be seen without performance,
held without condition,
loved without disguise.

It's safe here.
You don't have to hide anymore.

Morning Reflection:

Visibility without safety is trauma. I choose *safe* visibility.

Prompt:

- **Who in my life makes it safe to be seen — and how can I lean into that relationship?**

_____
_____
_____
_____
_____
_____
_____

Mindful Minute:

Close your eyes. Picture someone who sees you with love. Let their gaze soften your body.

Mantra:

"I can be seen and safe."

Evening Reflection:

- **Where did I feel emotionally safe today?**

_____
_____
_____
_____
_____
_____
_____

Day 76: The Mirror Is Not My Enemy

There were days you avoided your reflection,
not out of vanity, but out of pain.
The mirror felt like a confrontation —
with your failures, your wounds, your forgotten dreams.

But the mirror isn't your enemy.
It's an invitation.

To see not just what's on the surface,
but the man who's still becoming.
A man worthy of grace.
A man learning to belong to himself.

Morning Reflection:

The mirror doesn't judge — it reflects. But I do.

Prompt:

- What judgments do I project onto myself, and what is the gentler truth beneath them?

_____
_____
_____
_____
_____
_____
_____

Mindful Minute:

- Look at your reflection. Try to hold your gaze without criticism. Just witness.

_____
_____
_____
_____
_____
_____
_____

Mantra:

"I can look at myself with compassion."

Evening Reflection:

- **Did I offer myself kindness today — even when I felt unworthy?**

_____
_____
_____
_____
_____
_____
_____

Day 77: Seen and Still Loved

There were days you avoided your reflection—
not out of vanity, but out of quiet pain.
The mirror felt more like a reckoning—
with your failures, your wounds, your forgotten dreams.

But the mirror is not your enemy.
It's an invitation.

To see beyond the surface—
to meet the man still becoming.
A man worthy of grace.
A man learning to come home to himself.

Morning Reflection:

What if someone saw *everything* — and still stayed?

Prompt:

- **What part of me do I believe makes me unlovable — and what would change if I let someone see it?**

_____
_____
_____
_____
_____
_____
_____
_____

Mindful Minute:

Place both hands over your heart.

Whisper, "Even this version of me is worthy of love."

Mantra:

"I am worthy of being fully seen and fully loved."

Evening Reflection:

- **Did I practice radical self-acceptance today?**

_____
_____
_____
_____
_____
_____
_____

WEEK 12: The Masculine Need for Affection

Affection is not a weakness. It is oxygen. Too many men have been taught to crave it in silence, confuse it with sex, or reject it altogether. This week, we begin to unlearn the shame around tenderness and reintroduce ourselves to the sacred, necessary language of affection — beginning with self and moving outward.

Day 78 – Starved for Softness

You learned to survive on toughness—
stoicism, grit, the clenched jaw, the nod of "I'm fine."
But deep beneath the armor,
there's a quiet hunger you've rarely named:
the need for softness.

Not pity. Not weakness.
Just gentleness. Understanding.
The kind of softness that says:
"You don't have to prove anything here."

You weren't made to be hardened forever.
You were made to be held, too.

Morning Reflection:

I've been hardened by expectation, yet my heart still aches for warmth. I'm not broken for needing softness.

Prompt:

- **When was the last time I craved affection but felt ashamed to ask for it?**

_____
_____
_____
_____
_____
_____
_____
_____

Mindful Minute:

Wrap your arms around your torso and gently squeeze. Whisper, "I deserve this."

Mantra:

"Softness is not a threat — it's medicine."

Evening Reflection:

- **Did I notice or give myself a moment of softness today?**

_____
_____
_____
_____
_____
_____

Day 79 – When Touch Becomes Language

There are things words can't carry—
grief too old for syllables,
longing too deep for a sentence.

Sometimes, touch becomes the only language left.
A hand on your back that says, "I see you."
An embrace that melts years of guarded silence.
A steady palm reminding you that presence is enough.

You deserve that kind of language.
The one that speaks without asking you to explain.
The one that says:
You are worthy of tenderness.

Morning Reflection:

Touch speaks volumes. A shoulder squeeze, a hand held, a silent presence. I've missed these things more than I admit.

Prompt:

- **How do I feel about receiving or offering touch that isn't sexual?**

_____
_____
_____
_____
_____
_____
_____

- **Where do I resist it?**

_____
_____
_____
_____
_____
_____
_____

Mindful Minute:

Place your hand over your chest. Feel the rise and fall. Imagine it as a loved one's hand — steady, present.

Mantra:

"I welcome gentle connection."

Evening Reflection:

- **Did I experience physical or emotional closeness with someone today?**

_____
_____
_____
_____
_____
_____
_____
_____

Day 80 – I Wasn't Held, But I Can Learn

Maybe no one taught you how to hold pain—
not your own, not another's.
Maybe no one ever held you through your storms.
Only silence. Distance.
Survival.

But healing begins with new choices.
You can learn to be the arms you never had.
You can offer presence, where absence once lived.
You can soften, even when the world told you to harden.

This is not about blame.
It's about becoming the man
who knows how to hold—
with compassion, with patience, with love.

Morning Reflection:

I may not have grown up with much affection, but I can still learn how to give and receive it.

Prompt:

- **What kind of affection did I lack growing up — and how can I give it to myself now?**

_____
_____
_____
_____
_____
_____
_____

Mindful Minute:

Close your eyes and visualize someone holding you with love — no fixing, just presence.

Mantra:

"I am learning what love feels like."

Evening Reflection:

- **Did I reclaim a moment of nurturing today?**

_____
_____
_____
_____
_____
_____
_____

Day 81 – It's Not Always About Sex

Sometimes what you truly long for
isn't physical release—
but connection, closeness,
a feeling of being understood without having to perform.

The world often told you that touch, intimacy, and validation
must always lead to sex.
But what if it's deeper than that?

What if your body craves tenderness,
not conquest?
What if your heart wants to be heard,
not handled?

You are allowed to want warmth without expectation.
You are allowed to ask for presence,
not performance.

Morning Reflection:

Affection is not foreplay. It's connection. And I can want closeness without needing to earn it.

Prompt:

- **Where have I confused physical affection with performance or sexual obligation?**

_____
_____
_____
_____
_____
_____
_____

Mindful Minute:

Place one hand on your stomach and the other on your heart. Breathe into both spaces with intention.

Mantra:

"I can receive touch without expectation."

Evening Reflection:

- **Did I feel seen or embraced without pressure today?**

_____
_____
_____
_____
_____
_____
_____
_____

Day 82 – Words That Hold

Some words don't just fill silence—
they hold you.
Like a steady hand on your shoulder
when everything feels like it's falling apart.

Not every man grew up with words that soothed,
that named the ache,
that said, "I see you," without fixing you.

But you can change that.

You can speak to yourself with gentleness.
You can learn to say things that don't shrink you,
but ground you.
You can offer words that don't demand strength,
but allow softness.

Because the right words don't just land.
They stay.
They carry.

Morning Reflection:

Affection also lives in language. Words can hold me when arms cannot.

Prompt:

- What's the most healing thing someone has ever said to me?

_____
_____
_____
_____
_____
_____

Mindful Minute:

Repeat softly to yourself: **"You are worthy. You are loved. You are not too much."**

Mantra:

"Loving words are a form of holding."

Evening Reflection:

- **Did I give or receive a kind word today?**

Day 83: Affection Isn't Earned

You were taught to earn everything—
respect, rest, even love.
So when someone offers affection freely,
you hesitate,
wondering what you did to deserve it.

But affection isn't a reward.
It's not a medal for being strong,
or a prize for enduring quietly.

It's a basic human need.

And you don't have to perform pain
to receive it.
You don't have to shrink,
or strive,
or prove.

You are worthy of warmth,
even on your quiet days.
Especially then.

Morning Reflection:

I've distanced myself from the comfort of male closeness, but I can change that.

Prompt:

- **What stops me from expressing affection to the men in my life?**

_____
_____
_____
_____
_____
_____
_____
_____

- **Where did I learn that?**

_____
_____
_____
_____
_____
_____
_____
_____

Mindful Minute:

Send silent gratitude to a male friend, brother, mentor — someone you wish you could be softer with.

Mantra:

"Brotherhood can be tender."

Evening Reflection:

- **Did I allow space for meaningful connection with another man today?**

_____
_____
_____
_____
_____
_____
_____

Day 84: Holding Myself Isn't Sad — It's Sacred

There were nights you longed for arms
that never came.
So you learned to hold yourself—
in silence, in stillness,
in moments no one else noticed.

They might call it lonely.
But you know better.

To hold yourself with tenderness
isn't weakness.
It's a sacred act.
A quiet declaration
that you are worth the care
you were once denied.

This isn't sadness.
It's healing.
And it's holy.

Morning Reflection:

There's nothing pitiful about holding yourself. It's one of the bravest things a man can do.

Prompt:

- **How can I create a daily ritual of affection that starts with me?**

_____
_____
_____
_____
_____
_____
_____
_____

Mindful Minute:

Run your hands slowly down your arms, your face, your chest — not to fix, but to feel.

Mantra:

"Affection begins with me."

Evening Reflection:

- **Did I show myself love in a tangible way today?**

_____
_____
_____
_____
_____
_____
_____

WEEK 13: Guilt Around Wanting More

Many of us were taught that gratitude and desire cannot coexist — that wanting more meant we were ungrateful or selfish. But men are allowed to long, to hope, to grow beyond survival. This week, we sit with the discomfort of ambition and begin rewriting our permission slip to thrive.

Day 85: The Shame of Ambition

Somewhere along the line,
you were taught to shrink your hunger.
To silence your dreams
so you wouldn't come off as "too much."

Ambition became something to be ashamed of—
as though wanting more
meant being ungrateful for what you had.

But your desire to build,
to rise,
to become
is not arrogance.
It's aliveness.

There is no shame
in having a vision.
Only courage
in choosing to follow it.

Morning Reflection:

I've learned to shrink my dreams to avoid judgment. But I don't need to apologize for wanting more.

Prompt:

- **Where in my life do I feel guilty for wanting something better?**

_____
_____
_____
_____
_____
_____

Mindful Minute:

Close your eyes and visualize a life that feels free. Breathe into it — without shrinking it.

Mantra:

"It's okay to want more."

Evening Reflection:

- **Did I let myself hope out loud today?**

_____
_____
_____
_____
_____
_____
_____
_____

Day 86: Gratitude Doesn't Mean Settling

You can be thankful
and still want more.
Gratitude and growth
are not enemies.

They can hold hands—
one grounding you,
the other pulling you forward.

You don't have to settle
just because you're grateful.
Your contentment isn't a cage.

Let your gratitude be the soil,
not the ceiling.
You are allowed to bloom
beyond what you once prayed for.

Morning Reflection:

I can be deeply grateful and still desire growth. That's not a contradiction — it's truth.

Prompt:

- **Where have I used gratitude to silence my deeper desires?**

_____
_____
_____
_____
_____
_____
_____

Mindful Minute:

Place your hands on your chest and say, "I am thankful — and I am still becoming."

Mantra:

"Gratitude is a launch pad, not a prison."

Evening Reflection:

- **What did I appreciate today, and what do I still long for?**

_____
_____
_____
_____
_____
_____
_____

Day 87: Wanting Without Earning

You don't have to exhaust yourself
to deserve something good.

Love, rest, joy —
they are not wages.
They are birthrights.

The belief that you must suffer first
to receive
is not strength — it's survival mode.

You're allowed to want
without proving.
To desire
without apologizing.

You're worthy,
even in stillness.

Morning Reflection:

I don't have to earn peace, rest, or love. They are my birthrights, not rewards.

Prompt:

- **Where in my life do I feel like I need to "deserve" good things?**

_____
_____
_____
_____
_____
_____
_____
_____

Mindful Minute:

Repeat to yourself, slowly and deliberately: "I am already enough."

Mantra:

"I don't need to earn what I was born worthy of."

Evening Reflection:

- **Did I allow myself to receive without guilt today?**

_____
_____
_____
_____
_____
_____
_____
_____

Day 88: The Fear of Outgrowing Others

There's a quiet grief
that comes with growth —
the kind that whispers,
"If I change too much, will I still belong?"

You fear becoming unrelatable.
Too different. Too distant.
Like healing means leaving.

But evolving isn't betrayal.
It's honoring your becoming.

Some will grow with you.
Some won't.
But shrinking won't save the connection —
it'll only silence your soul.

Grow anyway.
You're not abandoning them.
You're returning to yourself.

Morning Reflection:

Sometimes we fear that healing means leaving people behind. That fear is real — but growth doesn't mean abandonment.

Prompt:

- **Who or what do I fear leaving behind if I change or grow?**

_____
_____
_____
_____
_____
_____
_____

Mindful Minute:

Breathe into your heart space.

Say: "It's safe for me to evolve."

Mantra:

"Growth is not betrayal."

Evening Reflection:

- **Did I shrink myself to stay familiar today?**

_____
_____
_____
_____
_____
_____
_____
_____

Day 89: Permission to Dream Again

Somewhere along the line,
you stopped dreaming.
Not because the dreams weren't real,
but because life convinced you
that dreaming was dangerous.

Too risky. Too fragile. Too much.

But you were never meant to live
only in survival mode.
You're allowed to want beauty,
to envision more than just getting by.

This is your permission slip:
to dream again,
to hope wildly,
to believe in a future
that feels like freedom.

Start small if you must —
but start.

Morning Reflection:

I've silenced many dreams to survive — but silence is not peace. I'm allowed to dream again.

Prompt:

- What dream did I bury to appear "realistic"?

_____
_____
_____
_____
_____
_____
_____

- What would it feel like to bring it back?

_____
_____
_____
_____
_____
_____

Mindful Minute:

Write down one old dream. Hold it in your hand. Just look. No fixing. Just remembering.

Mantra:

"My dreams are still alive."

Evening Reflection:

- **What forgotten part of me stirred today?**

_____
_____
_____
_____
_____
_____
_____
_____

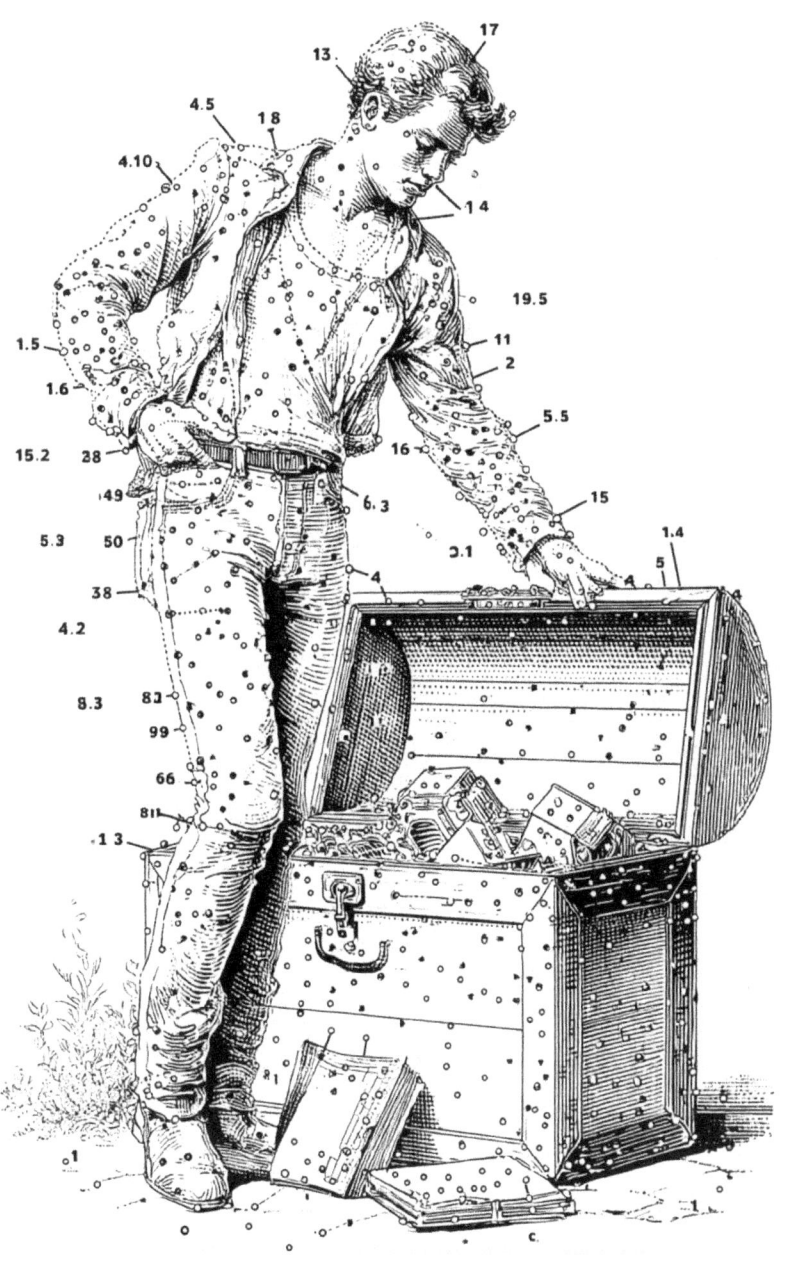

Day 90: The Guilt of Wanting Joy

There's a quiet guilt
that creeps in
when life finally gives you
a glimpse of joy.

As if happiness needs permission.
As if your past disqualifies you
from delight.

But joy isn't a betrayal
of where you've been.
It's a seed planted
in honor of your survival.

You don't have to earn it.
You only need to receive it.
Let it in —
without apology.

Morning Reflection:

Joy isn't selfish. It's sacred. And I don't need a reason to feel good.

Prompt:

- **What beliefs do I carry about joy?**

_____
_____
_____
_____
_____
_____
_____

- **Do I think it needs to be earned or justified?**

_____
_____
_____
_____
_____
_____
_____

Mindful Minute:

Close your eyes and smile — even if forced. Let your face relax. Let the idea of joy live there for a moment.

Mantra:

"I don't need a reason to smile."

Evening Reflection:

- **What moment of joy did I embrace — or resist — today?**

_____
_____
_____
_____
_____
_____
_____
_____

Month 3 Reflection: Hidden Wins

1. A Win I Haven't Celebrated Yet

- What did you accomplish that no one noticed—but mattered deeply to you?

_____
_____
_____
_____
_____
_____
_____
_____

Day 91: Reclaiming the "More" I Was Denied

You were taught to shrink —
to be grateful for crumbs,
to silence the ache for abundance
because "others have it worse."

But your longing is not greed.
It's memory.
It's your soul remembering
what you were made for.

Reclaim the "more" they said
wasn't for you.
Not out of entitlement,
but out of truth:
You were never meant to live
at the edge of your own life.

Morning Reflection:

Some of us were taught to survive, not thrive. But now, I get to choose differently.

Prompt:

- What does "more" look like for me — emotionally, mentally, spiritually?

_____
_____
_____
_____
_____
_____
_____

Mindful Minute:

With eyes closed, say softly: "This version of me deserves more." Breathe in that belief.

Mantra:

"I was made for more — and I won't apologize for it."

Evening Reflection:

- **Did I honor my hunger for more today?**

_____
_____
_____
_____
_____
_____
_____

WEEK 14:
How We've Been Taught to Abandon Ourselves

Self-abandonment doesn't always look like neglect. Sometimes, it looks like doing everything right for everyone else. This week is about recognizing the subtle ways we were conditioned to disconnect from ourselves — and reclaiming the right to come back home.

Day 92: When Pleasing Becomes Self-Erasure

At first, it felt like kindness —
making yourself small, agreeable, easy.
You just wanted peace.
Connection. Belonging.

But somewhere along the line,
pleasing became a performance.
You stopped asking, "What do I need?"
and only asked, "What do they expect?"

You don't have to disappear
to be loved.
True connection begins
when you stop editing yourself
just to be chosen.

Morning Reflection:

People-pleasing can feel noble — until I realize I'm disappearing in the process.

Prompt:

- **In what situations do I choose peace for others over peace for myself?**

_____
_____
_____
_____
_____
_____
_____

Mindful Minute:

Close your eyes. Say: "I deserve to take up space." Feel your body expand gently on the inhale.

Mantra:

"I can be kind without abandoning myself."

Evening Reflection:

- **Did I prioritize someone else's comfort over my own truth today?**

Day 93: Disconnection as Survival

You didn't mean to shut down.
It wasn't coldness. It was safety.
Sometimes, the only way to survive
was to feel nothing at all.

Disconnection wasn't your failure —
it was your armor.
A shield against the chaos,
the judgment, the pain.

But survival isn't the same as living.
And now, you're allowed to come back home
to your heart,
at your own pace.

Morning Reflection:

As a boy, I may have disconnected from my feelings to stay safe. But I don't have to keep surviving in the same ways.

Prompt:

- **What emotion did I learn to hide to stay "acceptable"?**

_____
_____
_____
_____
_____
_____
_____
_____

Mindful Minute:

Place your hand on your heart.

Say: "It's safe to feel." Stay there for three steady breaths.

Mantra:

"I can connect without fear."

Evening Reflection:

- **What emotion surfaced today that I usually avoid?**

_____
_____
_____
_____
_____
_____
_____

Day 94: Performing Strength, Abandoning Softness

You learned early that strength got applause —
and softness got silence.
So you flexed your resilience,
swallowed your tears,
and wore stoicism like a badge.

But in becoming the man they expected,
you betrayed the one you needed to be.

Softness isn't weakness.
It's the language of presence,
the birthplace of depth,
the doorway to healing.

You don't have to perform strength anymore.
You get to live it — gently.

Morning Reflection:

I was praised for being strong, not for being whole. But I don't need to perform anymore.

Prompt:

- **When do I pretend to be "fine" instead of being honest?**

_____
_____
_____
_____
_____
_____
_____

Mindful Minute:

Gently unclench your fists. Let your body relax fully — face, jaw, chest. Just be.

Mantra:

"My softness is not weakness."

Evening Reflection:

- **How did I show up more honestly today?**

_____
_____
_____
_____
_____
_____
_____

Day 95: Seeking Validation Outside Myself

You waited —
for the nod,
the affirmation,
the proof that you were enough.

You looked outward,
chasing applause,
approval,
affection.

But the truth is —
when you hand others the power
to name your worth,
you'll always feel small
in your own story.

It's time to return home —
to your voice,
your mirror,
your truth.

Let your own "yes" be enough.

Morning Reflection:

If I spend my life trying to prove myself to others, I'll always feel like I'm falling short.

Prompt:

- **Who have I tried to prove my worth to? What did it cost me?**

_____
_____
_____
_____
_____
_____
_____

Mindful Minute:

Stand or sit tall.

Say:

"I validate my own existence." Breathe with your spine straight and strong.

Mantra:

"I don't need external permission to be enough."

Evening Reflection:

- **Did I seek or offer myself validation today?**

_____
_____
_____
_____
_____
_____
_____

Day 96: When Boundaries Feel Like Betrayal

You were taught to give,
even when it emptied you.
To say "yes,"
even when your body whispered "no."

So now, when you draw a line—
it stings.
Not because you're wrong,
but because you were never taught
that self-respect isn't selfish.

You're not betraying anyone
by choosing peace.
You're learning
that love without boundaries
isn't love at all.

Morning Reflection:

Setting boundaries isn't betrayal. It's self-respect. And I'm allowed to choose myself.

Prompt:

- **Where in my life do I fear setting boundaries will make me look selfish?**

_____
_____
_____
_____
_____
_____
_____

Mindful Minute:

Say to yourself: "I can love others without losing myself." Breathe that truth into your body.

Mantra:

"Boundaries protect my becoming."

Evening Reflection:

- **Did I honor or override a boundary today?**

_____
_____
_____
_____
_____
_____
_____

Day 97: The Silence of Self-Neglect

It doesn't always look like breaking down.
Sometimes, it's quiet—
skipping meals, brushing things off,
shrinking your needs in rooms
where everyone else gets to take up space.

Self-neglect is the silence
between your own heartbeats.
The parts of you ignored,
because you thought they were too loud,
too much,
too inconvenient.

But you matter—
even when no one's watching.
Tend to yourself like someone worth caring for.
Because you are.

Morning Reflection:

Self-neglect isn't just physical. It's also emotional silence, spiritual disconnect, and mental fatigue.

Prompt:

- How do I ignore my own needs — and what need am I ready to finally hear?

_____
_____
_____
_____
_____
_____
_____

Mindful Minute:

Sit quietly and ask yourself, "What do I need right now?" Wait and listen.

Mantra:

"I am allowed to need."

Evening Reflection:

- Did I meet any of my needs today without guilt?

_____
_____
_____
_____
_____
_____
_____

Day 98: Coming Home to Myself

There is a kind of exhaustion
that doesn't come from work—
but from pretending, performing, and pleasing.

Today, I pause.
I take off the masks.
I stop shrinking to fit what the world demands.
I let myself be seen… by me.

Coming home to myself
isn't a destination.
It's a return—
again and again—
to the truth of who I am,
without apology.

Morning Reflection:

Coming home to myself means releasing the masks, the roles, the scripts.

Just being.

Just breathing.

Prompt:

- **What would coming home to myself look and feel like?**

_____
_____
_____
_____
_____
_____
_____
_____

Mindful Minute:

Close your eyes and say, "I am safe here — in me." Rest in that space for 60 seconds.

Mantra:

"I am returning to myself."

Evening Reflection:

- **What part of me felt most seen or reconnected today?**

_____
_____
_____
_____
_____
_____
_____
_____

WEEK 15: Stillness Is Power

This week invites you to slow down — not as weakness, but as reclamation. Stillness is not the absence of strength; it is its root. You are allowed to rest. You are allowed to pause. You are allowed to be.

Day 99: The Strength of Stillness

Stillness is not weakness.
It's not laziness, passivity, or surrender.

It's presence.

To sit with yourself—without the noise, without the rush—takes courage.
To feel what rises, to name it, to stay with it…
that's strength most people run from.

Today, I won't run.
I will be still.
And in that stillness, I'll remember:
I am not just what I do.
I am who I am becoming.

Morning Reflection:

Stillness doesn't mean I'm doing nothing — it means I'm listening. To my body. My truth. My breath.

Prompt:

- **What am I afraid I'll hear or feel when I slow down?**

_____
_____
_____
_____
_____
_____
_____

Mindful Minute:

Place one hand on your belly, one on your chest.

Breathe until your breath slows.

Just be here.

Mantra:

"Stillness is not weakness — it is where I meet my power."

Evening Reflection:

- **What truth did stillness help me notice today?**

_____
_____
_____
_____
_____
_____
_____
_____

www.ingramcontent.com/pod-product-compliance
Lightning Source LLC
Chambersburg PA
CBHW050254010526
44107CB00003B/313